SNOWDONIA WALKS FOR MOTORISTS

Northern Area

Warne Gerrard Guides for Walkers

Walks for Motorists Series

CHESHIRE WALKS

CHILTERNS WALKS
          Northern
          Southern

COTSWOLDS WALKS
          Northern
          Southern

JERSEY WALKS

LAKE DISTRICT WALKS
          Central
          Northern
          Western

LONDON COUNTRYSIDE WALKS
          North West
          North East
          South West
          South East

GREEN LONDON WALKS
          (both circular and cross country)

MIDLAND WALKS

NORTH YORK MOORS WALKS
          North and East
          West and South

PEAK DISTRICT WALKS

PENDLESIDE AND BRONTE COUNTRY WALKS

SNOWDONIA WALKS
          Northern

YORKSHIRE DALES WALKS

FURTHER DALES WALKS

Long Distance and Cross Country Walks

WALKING THE PENNINE WAY

RAMBLES IN THE DALES

Warne Gerrard Guides for Walkers

SNOWDONIA

WALKS FOR MOTORISTS
NORTHERN AREA

J. T. C. Knowles

30 circular walks
with sketch maps by
Robert Burns/Drawing Attention
8 photographs

FREDERICK WARNE

Published by
Frederick Warne (Publishers) Ltd
40 Bedford Square
London WC1B 3HE

The picture on the front cover shows the mountains near Llyn Ogwen and is reproduced by kind permission of Aberconwy Borough Council. The back cover shows the country between Cwm Penamnen and Blaenau Ffestiniog and was taken by W. W. Harris, as were the pictures of a shepherd and sheep in Snowdonia and of an old drovers' road. The pictures of Aberglaslyn Pass and of the view over Snowdon across Llyn Padarn appear by courtesy of the Snowdonia National Park Committee.

Publishers' Note
While every care has been taken in the compilation of this book, the publishers cannot accept responsibility for any inaccuracies. Things may have changed since the book was published: paths are sometimes diverted, a concrete bridge may replace a wooden one, stiles disappear. Please let the publishers know if you discover anything like this on your way.

The length of each walk in this book is given in miles and kilometres, but within the text Imperial measurements are quoted. It is useful to bear the following approximations in mind: 5 miles = 8 kilometres, $\frac{1}{2}$ mile = 805 metres, 1 metre = 39.4 inches.

ISBN 0 7232 2142 1
Phototypeset by Tradespools Ltd., Frome, Somerset
Printed by Galava Printing Co. Ltd., Nelson, Lancashire

Contents

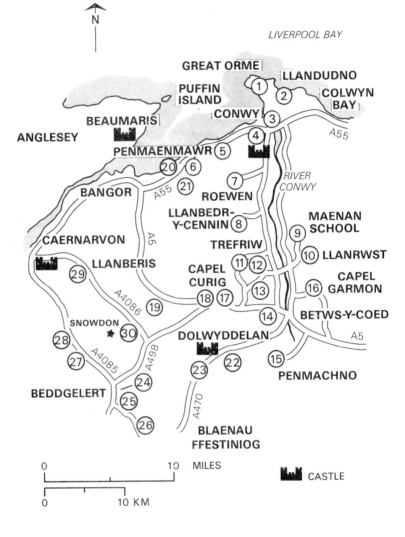

Introduction

The area of Snowdonia covered by these thirty circular walks includes some of the wildest and most spectacular scenery in England and Wales. The routes of these walks have, however, been chosen to pass through not only the mountainous region, but also to take in some of the outlying parts on the fringes of Snowdonia. This provides a tremendous variety of country to walk through – mountains, sea cliffs, river valleys, lakesides, forests and rural lanes – with much historical and natural historical interest as well as panoramic views of far distant hills and forests.

The walks have been planned to be, as far as possible, entirely circular and to vary between 3 and 10 miles in length, but, whilst only one or two are really strenuous, by the nature of the hilly country locally, the shorter distance walks are not always the easiest going ones, and the majority have stretches of uphill walking, which can be steep in places. The type of walk is described at the beginning of each route description so that some idea of the effort required can be gauged. Most, but not all, are suitable for all seasons of the year. Certainly those in the mountainous areas will need good waterproof boots, especially in the winter, and Walk 30, up Snowdon, should not be attempted except between May and October.

Since the walks are circular the start and finish are at the same spot, and the starting point for each has been chosen where there is a good car parking space and at an easy place to find for those new to the area. Many people find the Welsh place names rather daunting and difficult to follow. It is partly for this reason that Ordnance Survey map references are given with each walk, and for people unfamiliar with using the grid reference system an explanation of how to make use of it is given on p. 13. At the back of the book is a glossary of Welsh place names and their English translation. Other Welsh words commonly seen on signposts and public places are also included. In most cases, the Welsh style of place names has been used in this book, in line with the Ordnance Survey Maps of Wales, e.g. Llyn for Lake, and Afon for River.

The routes of all the walks are over public rights of way or along country lanes and roads. Footpaths across farmland should be kept to and, needless to say, on those lanes without a footpath, although it is very unlikely that much traffic will be met with, even on the busiest of bank holidays, it is important to take care, as many are narrow and winding.

Hopefully, the route descriptions and sketch maps of the walks will be quite clear, if carefully followed. For those paths within the Gwydyr and Beddgelert Forest areas it is certainly vital to keep to the route described, as in the forests there is a maze of unmetalled roads, built for timber hauling, and it is very easy to loose one's way if the routes are not followed exactly.

It is also important to observe the country code, as this helps to keep good relations between those who come to enjoy the country and those who earn their living from it. The country code is given below and all walkers are asked to observe it.

> Guard against fire risk.
> Fasten all gates.
> Keep dogs under proper control.
> Keep to the paths across farmland.
> Avoid damaging fences, hedges and walls.
> Leave no litter.
> Safeguard water supplies.
> Protect wild life, wild plants and trees.
> Go carefully on country roads.
> Respect the life of the countryside.

For those who want to take their dogs with them, it is necessary to remember that the country and hills in North Wales are widely used for sheep rearing, so it is particularly important that dog owners make sure that their dogs do not worry the sheep in any way. Farmers have wide powers to take strong measures against dogs caught worrying sheep. Against each walk, notes are given as to its suitability for dogs from this point of view. In fact, the best places for dogs to run loose are on those routes taking in Forestry Commission land where, generally, no livestock is grazed and dogs can roam without the worry of their troubling sheep.

As none of the walks reaches the highest parts of the more pre-cipitous mountains, the equipment required need not be elaborate. A good pair of walking shoes, or boots, is absolutely essential, especially out of the summer season. Not all the routes are over dry ground and, from autumn to spring especially, patches of boggy ground will certainly be met with. A good thick pair of woollen socks also helps for more comfortable walking in these conditions. Wet weather clothing should always be carried. Even on the lower slopes above 1000 ft (305 m) the weather can be quite different from that in the valleys, or near to the coast – cooler and sometimes wetter, and it can change very rapidly. Many people who do get caught out on the hills without adequate protective clothing find how quickly these conditions can become alarming. A compass is not only a safeguard but is handy for helping to identify from the map far distant features from a particular view point. Similarly a pair of binoculars is useful and should give added enjoyment to the walk.

Finally, it is suggested, that whilst all the walks are well within the capabilities of most active people and none is really strenuous, it would perhaps be better to tackle the shorter, easier walks first. It is surprising how soon the out of condition motorist becomes able to cope with the longest walk, after a short 'warming-up' period. For the ardent walker, no apology is made for including some of the shorter walks, as they are all worth following and each, as far as possible, gives a good variety of scenery and terrain, and includes features of special interest.

Notes on the area

The roughly square area covered by these walks takes in the North Wales coast from Bangor to Colwyn Bay, then its boundary runs southwards down the Conwy Valley to Pentrefoelas, turning westwards to Blaenau Ffestiniog and Beddgelert and then northwards to Caernarvon. The majority of this block of country lies within the Snowdonia National Park. This area was designated a National Park in 1951 and covers 845 square miles. It contains Snowdon, at 3560 ft (1085 m) the highest mountain in England and Wales, and also thirteen other peaks above 3000 ft (914 m) almost all located in the northern half of the Park. These peaks, except Snowdon, are all only accessible by fairly arduous walking and climbing, consequently the ascent of most of them is not within the scope of this book.

The hills, mountains, rivers, lakes and forests provide not only recreation for people with many different interests, but also employment for a relatively large number of people: they are the heartland of Wales. This country by its remoteness and character has always been the stronghold of the Welsh, and earlier inhabitants, against successive waves of invaders. These came mostly from the east but also, in the final stages of the Roman occupation during the fourth and fifth centuries, from Ireland and the west. On its eastern edge, the highlands of the Denbigh moors and the river Conwy must have proved natural barriers to all invading armies and tribes moving westwards from what is now Cheshire and Shropshire.

With this very varied and long history, reaching back through medieval times to the Iron and Bronze ages, there are naturally a great number of relics – dolmens, cairns, cromlechs, standing stones, castles and ancient buildings – to be found throughout the area. The Ordnance Survey map marks some of these sites, especially those that have been properly excavated and studied, but on these walks, and in driving around, it will be clear that many ancient places, especially standing stones and tumuli, are not marked down.

In the earlier days, before the Romans came in 46 AD most of the dwellings and villages were near to the top of the hills, to judge by where most of the remains of the huts and graves of this period are found. It is thought that the lower parts of the valleys would have been too swampy and unhealthy to be lived in safely, being overgrown with thick woods and the haunt of wild animals. It is likely, also, that the winters were warmer, making the hills more habitable than now. Nowadays snow lies on the north-facing slopes of some of the higher peaks well into May each year.

Clearance of the woods would have started after the introduction of tools of stone, bronze or iron, and gradually man would have moved down into the valleys. The changes in this pattern of life are well reflected in the remains to be found. Most of the knowledge of how the people lived from day to day prior to the Wars of the Roses is conjecture based on the remains found, the few brief comments about North Wales made by the Romans and later by travelling friars and monks, and also what can be gleaned from the Welsh literature remaining from those times. However, the pattern of life is unlikely to have changed much up to the Industrial Revolution of the eighteenth century.

The Romans first came in 46 AD and remained in the area for about 300 years, but, unlike the more southerly and eastern parts of Britain, North Wales was never truly Romanized. The Romans came here for the purpose of defending the outer perimeter of Britain and to exploit the minerals already known to exist, rather than for colonization. The copper mines on the Great Orme, Llandudno, the gold in central Wales, and the lead mines around Betws-y-Coed and Llanrwst were probably all in use during the Roman occupation. The Romans were also interested in the pearls found in the large freshwater mussels living in the river Conwy near to Trefriw and Caerhun. This famous industry, like the lead and copper mines, is now finished, very few of the big mussels being left.

Apart from farming, mining is certainly the oldest industry of the area. Copper mines existed in Bronze Age times on the Great Orme and on the other hills in Snowdonia and they were worked until about a hundred years ago. Llandudno, prior to 1850, was a poor mining community perched on the side of the Great Orme.

Lead, likewise, has been mined since early times, but reached its heyday in the seventeenth and eighteenth centuries. The last mine, near Llanrwst, finally closed down about twenty years ago. Quarrying for limestone, slate, and granite has also been a major source of employment, but once again, these industries have shrunk. However, unlike the mining, quarrying is still important on a smaller scale, especially for granite and slate. Stone Age man knew the value of the granite found near to Penmaenmawr on the coast. A stone age 'axe factory' has been discovered above Penmaenmawr, where about 5000 years ago man used the special stone there for making axe heads. These rough, unpolished heads were polished elsewhere and Penmaenmawr axes have been found all over England, and northern Europe. Many axe head rejects are still to be found on the slopes of where the 'axe factory' was. Examples of all these relics of past activities can be seen on many of the walks described, and they indicate the changes in pattern of life in the area.

Nowadays hill farming and forestry with some fishing and quarrying are the main activities of people concerned with gaining a living from the area in the traditional pattern. Tourism, service industries, and to a limited extent, modern factories have superseded the older ways of life, but this newer style of employment has tended to concentrate people in the coastal towns or around existing villages and towns on the main road routes. The more outlying places are in decline and many ruined cottages and farms will be seen on the walks – an indication of days when people were more widespread through the area.

The great variety of country in the region covered by these walks is reflected in the variety of animal and plant life found there. The routes for the walks have been chosen with this in mind, so as to provide not only good walking, but also to give a chance to discover as much of the local natural history as possible.

Bird life is particularly rich and varied through the area, the sea, headlands, rivers, forests and uplands all providing different habitats with their characteristic species. On the coast, in the summer, the great headlands of the Great and Little Ormes, Penmaenbach and Penmaenmawr are the haunt of thousands of nesting sea birds – fulmars, guillemots, razorbills, cormorants, shags, and kittiwakes, as well as each headland having its resident pairs of ravens and the occasional peregrine falcon. Outside the breeding season, these high cliffs are quiet except for the herring gulls and jackdaws. At these times, however, many flocks of ducks can usually be seen just out to sea, especially red-breasted mergansers, goldeneye and scoters, with the occasional visiting red-throated diver and parties of grebes (great crested and black-necked).

The Conwy Estuary, in summer, is relatively deserted, except for several hundred shelducks, a few herons, and parties of terns and gulls. Sandwich terns are particularly common on the Conwy side of the mouth of the river Conwy. Later, in August and September, a passage of waders begins and lapwings, dunlin, ringed plover, redshank, oyster-catchers, curlew and turnstones are regularly seen, with smaller groups of knots, sanderling, grey plover and greenshank. Here, though, the unusual can occur at any time of the year.

The upland rivers, fast flowing and clear, invariably provide the walker with a view of a dipper or two and of grey wagtails. Each stretch of even the smallest rivers seems to have its resident pairs of these two species. Kingfishers are found more regularly on the slower flowing, deeper parts of the bigger rivers, whilst, in summer, sandpipers are found around the edges of most of the lakes.

In the forests, especially Gwydyr, a new population is slowly building up of birds typical of coniferous forests: black grouse, crossbills, lesser redpolls, siskins and goldcrests are all regularly to be seen, as well as buzzards and ravens. On the open hills of the east the haunting, bubbling, cry of the curlew can be heard throughout the summer, for these deserted hills are the breeding grounds for many curlews, as well as redshanks and lapwings. Of the smaller birds, stonechats and redstarts are frequently found; and in the remnants of the oak woods along the valleys, especially around Betws-y-Coed and at Aber, pied flycatchers and wood warblers are common.

This brief account of the birds to be found here only picks out the more unusual or typical species at each place, but, on any one walk, an enthusiast with a pair of binoculars should be able to see thirty to forty different species, which is an indication in itself of the wide variety of bird life to be found.

Animals, unlike birds, are less often seen but there is an equally wide variety which can be spotted during daytime even if only as a fleeting glimpse. The largest and certainly easiest to watch are the wild goats on the Great Orme and some of the Snowdonia mountains. These are descendants of tame goats that escaped, or were let loose, between one and two hundred years ago. In the distance the goats look like sheep but are generally creamier in colour, more angular in shape and, of course, the billies have very large horns. Another large animal that can often be seen from the Great Orme is the grey seal. Solitary seals regularly swim around the base of the cliffs of the Ormes at all times of the year. None breed here, Puffin Island being the nearest spot, but they fairly regularly visit the Ormes, and can be watched easily from the Marine Drive.

Strangely, deer are no longer found in the area, although red deer were recorded in the seventeenth century around Roewen.

Badgers are present, judging by the number of setts, but they very rarely come out in the daytime. Foxes are more likely to be seen during the day and, in the remoter hills and lanes, can often be surprised, or be seen crossing the paths. Stoats and weasels are also most often seen on the lanes, the dry stone walls being a fine refuge for them. Their larger relative the polecat is fairly common in North Wales, and in the forest areas there is a good chance of briefly catching a glimpse of one – often looking like a short legged, black cat streaking across the path. The much rarer pine marten keeps to the deeper forest areas around Betws-y-Coed, and anyone seeing one is very lucky. Their prey, grey squirrels, are very common, unlike the red squirrel which is still on the decline and is now very rare throughout this part of Wales.

Hares and rabbits are, on the other hand, on the increase, in spite of myxomatosis, and it is now quite normal to see either species anywhere. Similarly, moles and hedgehogs are very common. This is shown by the lines of molehills threading their way through even the rockiest meadows, quite high up in the hills, and by the numbers of dead hedgehogs on the roads in the autumn.

Snakes and lizards (mostly the non-poisonous grass snakes and the common lizard) are about in the summer, lizards especially enjoying a warm day on the stone walls. There are very few adders in the area. The grass snakes feed on the many local frogs, and frog spawn can be found in ponds and ditches everywhere early in the year. Semi-palmate newts are also quite widespread in some of the ponds and pools, especially around Llandudno.

The walker with a sharp eye will certainly see many birds and wild animals on any one of the thirty walks in this book.

Plants of the area could be the subject of a whole book as the variety and number of rare species is very great. On every one of these walks the botanist should be able to find plants which are listed as rarities in Britain – be careful not to pick them. The lanes and hedges on the eastern side of the Conwy are particularly rich and colourful in the spring and summer, as is the country behind Llandudno, known as the Creuddyn Peninsula.

No attempt has been made to describe in detail or help to identify the species of wild life to be found, as it is not within the scope of this book. The Observer's Series are of an especially handy size and weight for carrying around, and give a comprehensive on the spot guide to identifying any birds, animals, plants and butterflies seen.

Ordnance Survey Map References

At the beginning of each walk in this book the Ordnance Survey map reference for the starting place is given, to help the reader locate the area of the walk. Some walks also have map references in the text where there is a possibility of confusion along the way.

Ordnance Survey maps of the 1:50,000 series (1 cm to $\frac{1}{2}$ km) are over printed with a grid system in blue running in a north–south and east–west direction. Around the border of the map are a series of numbers in blue against each line of the grid.

To find a particular place on the map, generally six numbers are given, the first three refer to numbers running across the top and bottom of the map from left to right, and the second set of three numbers refer to the numbers running up either side of the map.

Each set of three numbers is made up as follows: the first two refer to the printed number and the third gives an indication of how far across the grid square one has to go, e.g. in 785, 78 refers to the printed blue number in the margin and the 5 indicates that the place is half way across that square. By working the second set of three numbers in a similar way one can fairly accurately pinpoint on the map a particular place referred to in the text. For example on sheet No. 115 (Caernarvon and Bangor) the end of Llandudno pier has a grid reference of 785833.

The areas where these walks are located are covered by three Ordnance Survey maps in the 1:50,000 series. The majority of the walks are shown on sheet 115 (Caernarvon and Bangor). The exceptions are: Walk 26, sheet 124 (Dolgellau); Walk 16, sheet 116 (Denbigh and Colwyn Bay); and Walks 2, 3, 9 and 10, sheets 115 *and* 116.

Walk 1   The Great Orme, Llandudno

3 miles (5 km)

Start: the summit of the Great Orme, OS map ref. 768834

This walk commences at the highest point of the Great Orme (679 ft, 207 m) and follows a route across the top of the headland before joining the Marine Drive, which from the footpath has spectacular views along the North Wales coast and the sea cliffs. There is a wide variety of bird and plant life to be seen at all times of the year, as well as a considerable amount of historical interest on the way. Once at the summit car park, the going is fairly easy.

The country is limestone heathland and sheep graze freely across it. Dogs should be kept under control for the whole route.

The summit of the Great Orme can be reached by car, taking the very steep road up past the Empire Hotel at the end of Mostyn Street in Llandudno, and then following the road up beside the tram track. Alternatively a more enjoyable route during May to October is to park in the town close to the tram station and take the tram to the summit. The trams run frequently and the return fare is modest. They were built in 1902 and are a feature of the town.

The King's Head, which is just above the tram station, is the inn where Llandudno, as a resort, was first planned in 1848. Prior to this the town was a poor farming and mining community working the vein of copper which runs through the carboniferous limestone of the Great Orme. Another possibility is to take the cable car to the summit. This is a 9 minute ride on the longest cable car system in Britain, leaving from close to the end of the pier. Cars can be parked in Llandudno.

Commencing at the Summit Hotel, which is now no longer a hotel but contains a bar and a café, walk up the small hill behind it towards the cable car station. At the top of this hillock there is a marker. There are views of the coast eastwards as far as Liverpool and the Mersey; further to the north on clear days the Lancashire coast and parts of Cumbria can be seen. Due north, the Isle of Man is sometimes visible as a dark smudge on the horizon, and southwards the mountains of Snowdonia rise up, range upon range.

From the marker walk downhill towards the cart track. The pasture on one's left is notable for the ridges in it, showing up especially clearly in the evening light. These are the remains of a medieval field system where strips of land were cultivated either by different individuals or for different crops. Joining the stony track turn left and walk along it. After about 700 yards the track runs alongside a

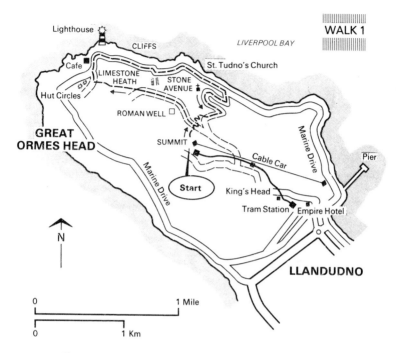

Lighthouse

CLIFFS

LIVERPOOL BAY

Cafe

St. Tudno's Church

LIMESTONE HEATH

STONE AVENUE

Hut Circles

ROMAN WELL

GREAT ORMES HEAD

SUMMIT

Marine Drive

Pier

Cable Car

Start

King's Head

Marine Drive

Tram Station

Empire Hotel

N

LLANDUDNO

0   1 Mile

0   1 Km

stone wall on the left. Keep on beside this wall and after about ¼ mile, a small spring in the wall is reached – Ffynon Llygaid. This has recently been surrounded by some modern stonework but it is, in fact, recorded as being in use in Roman times, and is called the 'Roman well'. Continue along the track. About 200 yards further on, clumps of gorse start to grow on the right hand side.

Turning off the track here and walking for about 100–200 yards through these clumps of gorse towards the sea, one comes to a Neolithic stone avenue, known as Hwylfa'r Ceirw (literally the Path of the Deer). This avenue leads from an ancient square stone enclosure and runs down towards the cliff edge. It has never been excavated and is assumed to be a Bronze Age ceremonial avenue, though for what purpose is not known. Returning to the track, continue along it up to the point where the wall takes a sharp left hand bend. At this corner, keep straight on across the heath. This area is notable for its limestone pavements, expanses of bare rock which have deep cracks and holes in them, known as grikes. Many moisture-loving plants and especially ferns find refuge from being grazed by sheep and goats and protection from the wind in these gullies.

Walking across the heath bear slightly to the left and after ¼ mile, a concrete road is reached. This is part of the remains of old wartime fortifications when many coastal artillery batteries were installed here

15

to protect the approaches to the Mersey and Liverpool and for gunnery training. Turn right down this concrete road until it reaches the Marine Drive. At the junction of the road and the Marine Drive, on the left, is a patch of grass-covered ground and on the far side of this ground, partially hidden in the bracken in the summer, are the outlines of a series of hut circles of the Bronze Age. These may date from 1000 BC making them in all 3000 years old. The base of these ancient houses would have been dug into the ground and edged with stones, and this is what remains. The roof would have been made of wood and covered with turves, bracken and other natural, easily obtainable materials.

Turn right down the Marine Drive, past the Rest and Be Thankful refreshment kiosk and walk for about a mile. This stretch gives a magnificent view of the sea cliffs, and in the spring and summer there will be excellent views of the fulmars, kittiwakes, cormorants, shags, guillemots and razorbills all of which come to nest on the cliffs – not to mention the resident herring gulls, jackdaws, and ravens. A passing peregrine falcon may sometimes be seen on this stretch and, in winter, off shore, various seabirds can be seen – divers, ducks and grebes. Grey seals regularly visit the Orme and swim along the base of the cliffs, whilst on the slopes above the Marine Drive the Great Orme herd of wild goats often congregates. The Marine Drive continues past the entrance to the lighthouse – one of the few in the country where husband and wife can live together – the lighthouse is more than 300 feet above sea level and helps to guide the shipping into the Mersey. On a clear day, one can see many ships of all types passing around the north of Anglesey to and from Liverpool.

A road junction is eventually reached. Take the zig-zag road to the right up the hill, past St Tudno's Church, and the Old Rectory tea gardens. The church is the original church of the area and was where St Tudno had his monastic cell. Passing by the church walk up the grassy slope to the Summit. This last part is fairly steep but by following a zig-zag sheep track the climb is made much easier.

Walk 2   Nant-y-Gamar and Penrhynside

3¾ miles (6 km)

Start: the County Hotel, Craig-y-Don, OS map ref. 795822

This walk passes through the area known as the Creuddyn Peninsula, which is that piece of land jutting out into the Irish sea, with the Great Orme at its tip, and with Llandudno, and the villages of Deganwy and Craig-y-Don also lying on it. The main A55 road from Chester to Conwy is at the neck of this peninsula. Although the area would seem to be very built up, in fact, most of the houses are around the outer edges and in the centre there are still fine areas of open country and woods, which provide some excellent walking. There are several SSSIs (Sites of Special Scientific Interest) on the peninsula and also it is full of historical places. This walk is easy going and only passes through relatively few areas of sheep pasture. It is, therefore, suitable for allowing dogs to run freely. However, care should be taken not to allow dogs to chase the pheasants, during the breeding season especially, as many of the woods are used for the raising of pheasants in natural conditions, and are private property.

There is plenty of car parking space in the Craig-y-Don area. Starting at the County Hotel on the sea front at Craig-y-Don, walk through the small shopping area, directly away from the sea. Keep straight across the cross-roads and go down Queen's Road. Several residential roads run off to the left and right and Queen's Road passes a small park on the left, with a public bowling green and tennis courts on the right. After about ½ mile turn left into Fferm Bach road. Rapallo House Museum is on the left, a short distance up the hill. This museum is well worth a visit, having a sizeable collection of paintings, Welsh furniture and local finds.

Carry on past Rapallo House up the short steep hill, and at its brow, just past the rear lodge to Lady Forester's Home, there is a stony track to the right. Lady Forester's was a convalescent home for women from Manchester, but has now been bought by a consortium of doctors to be converted into a private medical centre. The path runs past Tan-yr-Allt (Under the Hillside) cottage and over a stone stile. The cliffs on the left are interesting in that, being of limestone, they have many ledges and cracks. Herring gulls and jackdaws nest on them, and also fulmars. It is rare for the fulmar to nest even a mile or two inland, since it is mainly a marine bird, related to the albatross. In June and July red valerian covers these cliffs. The path passes through low scrubby woods behind an old farm. On the left the remains of an old lime kiln can still be seen. Limestone was roasted in the kiln to form lime for use on the fields. The small quarry that was used to feed

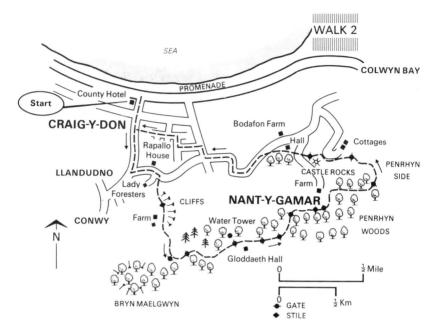

the kiln is still there, full of ferns of different types, especially the hart's tongue fern.

Shortly after the kiln, the path comes out into the open. In late summer, this area is bright with the spectacular, yellow mullein. Ahead and slightly to the right is a wooded hill – Bryn Maelgwyn. The path runs towards it along a fence and then, just before a swing gate, turns sharp left up a grassy slope. This area of grassland, although grazed heavily by sheep, is very rich in limestone plants, some of which are rare: thyme, madder, squill, rockrose and sandwort.

Pass through a kissing gate into a wood of oak, elm, sycamore, and hawthorn. There is also a fine stand of yew trees on the left. This is an excellent area to see many different species of woodland birds, as well as squirrels and hares. There is a badger sett on Bryn Maelgwyn. Follow the path through the wood onto a stony track running beside a high wall on the right. The limestone rocks used to build this wall are full of fossil remains of shellfish. On the left the flowers growing on the small limestone slab of rock attract many butterflies in the summer, this being a warm and secluded spot. The path bears slightly left through another swing gate and runs along between a high wall and the wood.

Gloddaeth Hall stands behind this wall and was the home of the Mostyn family from Tudor times until recently. It is now a boy's boarding school – St David's College. An old water tower stands in the wood along this part of the path, together with some magnificent holm oaks. At the end of the grounds of Gloddaeth Hall, the path bears left through another kissing gate. From here there are views across the open fields towards Colwyn Bay and Rhos Church, which stands out prominently on a hill.

Keeping up the hill at the edge of the wood, pass through another gate. This section of the wood always seems to attract plenty of nuthatches, jays, goldcrests, tits of various types, treecreepers and woodpeckers. Following the path up through the wood, it eventually comes out onto Nant-y-Gamar hill. This is another fine area of limestone grassland, with outcrops of limestone pavement rich in flowers. In the summer, stonechats, wheatears and sometimes ring ousels can be seen here.

Coming out of the wood, turn sharp right and follow the wall. At the end of the open grassland area the path leads through another kissing gate into a more wooded area. Keep straight on and through another gate. Turn sharp left here up a series of limestone steps. At the top, a small farm can be seen on the left, and at this point turn right, following the path through Penrhynside Woods. High gorse bushes line the path, with occasional open patches. Spotted orchids, as well as rarer orchid species can be seen here in late spring and summer. Crossing a small clearing the path leads into an oak wood, with a further kissing gate at the end of it. Carrying straight on along this path leads into Penrhynside village – where there are a couple of pubs – but, if a diversion is made, return to this gate, as the route of the walk turns sharp left immediately through the gate and up the grassy hill alongside the wood. Follow the track across the side of the hill and, as the ground rises, there is on clear days a fine view of the mountains of Snowdonia, especially the Carneddau and the hump backed shape of Moel Siabod. Ahead lies the sweep of Llandudno Bay, bounded by the Great Orme, whilst to the left, Anglesey and Puffin Island can be clearly seen. The hillside on the right is covered in gorse but is also rich in harebells, campion, thyme and heather. Stonechats, linnets and whitethroats are common here, as well as kestrels and sparrow hawks, and the occasional merlin.

Keeping the hedge on your left a narrow path is reached, passing a ruined cottage and running between two hedges. This path leads to another gate. Bear left and pass by a small settlement of houses. One of these has clearly been a chapel, an indication of the times when this was a distinct community, the chapel serving all the scattered cottages and farms near by. Many of these are now derelict or only used at week-ends in the summer. The path runs down to the access road to the cottages, which a few yards further on turns downhill in a hairpin bend. On the bend, take the path straight across towards Llandudno. This goes through a gate and carries on past an outcrop of rocks on the left known locally as 'Castle Rocks'. The cracks in these rocks are full of ferns of many different species. Cross the concrete farm track towards Craig-y-Don and carry on into the woods.

The path leads downhill, behind Bodafon Hall (built in 1610), where one can get tea and coffee. A good view of the layout and buildings of the old established Bodafon Farm can be had from this path. The path reaches Bodafon Road, carry on down the lane towards Llandudno. This is the old road across to Penrhynside from Deganwy, and at the end of the last century an inscribed, early Christian stone of about AD 600 was found on the southern side of the road just beyond Bodafon Hall. This stone is now kept at Llanrhos Church.

Passing a quarry with a small electricity sub-station in it, a cross roads is reached. Turn right down towards the sea, then left into St Margaret's Drive, and through the small park to the centre of Craig-y-Don and the County Hotel on the sea front.

Walk 3   Deganwy Castle and Llanrhos

5½ miles (9 km)

Start: Deganwy Church, OS map ref. 783791

Another part of the Creuddyn Peninsula is covered by this walk. It provides a longer route than either of the previous two. The going is fairly easy and good at all times of the year through a variety of country. There is great historical interest at Deganwy Castle and at Bodysgallen Hall. Early on there is a stretch of sheep pasture, but, after that, the walk is suitable for taking dogs.

Starting at Deganwy Church, where there is a good sized car park, go through the gate and up the gravelled path. After 100 yards, turn left up the grassy hill towards a stile over a wire fence. This grassy area is notable for the rare maiden pinks which flower in profusion in June, July and August – they are not for picking. Climb the stile and walk up towards a gap in the rocks at the brow of the hill. From here, the two hills of Deganwy Castle will be seen straight ahead across the sheep pasture. Walk straight across the pasture to the saddle between these two hills.

These twin hills have been fortified for hundreds of years, most likely since the time when Irish invaders started to overrun this area at the end of the Roman occupation in the fourth and fifth centuries AD.

There are very few remains of the castle left, for it was demolished by Llewellyn ap Iorwerth in 1263, but some small sections of wall can still be seen. Both hills were fortified but the main castle was on the left hand one nearest to the sea. The saddle in the middle was a walled-in compound for the horses and, possibly, a protected area for the serfs and villagers. Deganwy Castle is known to have been occupied by the Welsh Princes in the sixth century, and possibly, earlier by the Romans.

The Normans had a wooden walled castle here, held by Baron Hugh (the Wolf), and in the twelfth and thirteenth centuries it was the scene of bitter fighting, not only between the Welsh and English but also between rival Welsh princes. King John in 1211 and King Henry III in 1245 both came here and occupied the castle, camping on the open area around it. The English armies generally were exhausted by the time they reached Deganwy after making their way across the wild country from Chester or Shrewsbury and often had to retire with heavy losses due to lack of food and the guerilla tactics of the Welsh. The main entrance to the castle ran spirally around the left hand hill, allowing the defenders to attack the besiegers as they made their way up the hill under the ramparts.

At the top, where there are fine views of the Conwy estuary,

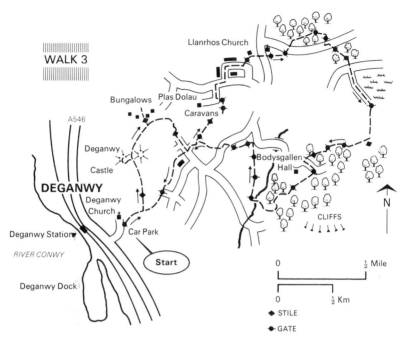

Llanrhos Church

Bungalows Plas Dolau

A546

Caravans

Deganwy

Castle

Bodysgallen
Hall

DEGANWY

Deganwy
Church

Deganwy Station

CLIFFS

N

RIVER CONWY

Car Park

Start

0   ½ Mile

Deganwy Dock

0   ½ Km

◆ STILE

●─ GATE

Anglesey and Snowdonia, a large hollow can still be seen. This was the dungeon, and it is known that in the thirteenth century at least one Welsh prince was held prisoner in this dungeon for many years by a rival prince. Retracing the path to the saddle between the hills, walk to the far side, where there is the solitary remains of part of the wall. Here the old town of Gannock stood in the shelter of the castle, and it is still possible to see the shape of the foundations of various long houses in this area.

Walk across the pasture towards the bungalows. A stile is reached leading down between two of the houses; do not cross this, but turn right and walk up the hedge at the end of the gardens. After 200–300 yards a finger post is reached; keep straight on bearing slightly right around a knoll, until the grass covered remains of an old field wall is reached. Follow this down past a very small pond to a gate and a public footpath finger post. Climb the wooden stile and carry on down the narrow bridle path, which widens into a lane further down. There is a caravan camp in the field on the left. At the bottom, bear left up a path between the caravans and a large house standing on a hill. This path crosses the entrance to Bwlch Farm Caravan Site, and continues across the fields towards another caravan site. Climb the stile, cross the ditch and bear half right through the middle of the caravan site. At the other side of this field is a public footpath finger post and a kissing gate. Go through and turn left along the hedge. At the end of this hedge there is another gate leading onto the driveway to Plas Dolau Farm. Walk to the entrance of the drive and turn right down the road. Take the first turning left, down a small residential road (Hill View Road) then turn right past some more modern houses. After 200–300 yards a footpath on the left between two of the houses leads across the fields to the Deganwy to Llandudno road and Llanrhos Church.

Cross the main road, and on the far side of the small church car park, go through an archway and follow a line of concrete marker posts across the meadow towards the woods. Bryn Maelgwyn lies to the left. Llanrhos Church is the original parish church for a large area, covering Deganwy, Llandudno Junction and parts of Craig-y-Don. First mentioned in 1282, it was on the site of a much older wooden building. At one time an inn – the Mostyn Arms – on the main road flanked the church, but Lady Mostyn, in late Victorian times, not thinking this 'seemly' had it pulled down.

At the far side of the meadow, cross over the drive to St David's College (Gloddaeth Hall) and follow the path through the woods. There is a large badger's sett on the hillside, and characteristic badger tracks through the undergrowth of the wood radiate from here – badgers tending to follow the same paths every night. After about $\frac{1}{4}$ mile, a gate is reached at the end of the wood, which leads into a meadow, with a large modern house built in one corner. At the middle of the meadow turn right and walk to the driveway to Gloddaeth Hall, where there is a gate and public footpath finger post. Walk along the drive for a few yards and then on the right go downhill across the fields through another gate. Follow the concrete marker posts half left, which bring the path out at Glanwydden Lane (OS map ref. 804802). Cross over, taking care as this lane, for its size, carries a lot of traffic. The cart track opposite bears left between high hedges. This low lying area is a favourite haunt of reed buntings.

A field gate is reached; pass through and walk straight across the field to the corner of another field, follow the hedge up the hill, and then cut across towards the woods, after passing through a field gateway. Crossing the field, a stile can be seen half left at the edge of the wood. Walk to the stile, do not climb it, but turn right and walk diagonally across to the far corner of the same field. Pass through the gateway to the corner of another wood. A swing gate leads onto a path along the edge of the wood; climb over a stile, cross the head of a meadow, and as the path enters a stand of trees scramble up the bank. Horses use this path and the bank can be rather muddy and slippery in wet weather. At the top bear right and walk to a stone stile over a wall.

Bodysgallen Hall is straight ahead. This was another of the homes of the Mostyn family. Built in Jacobean times on the site of a much older building, it has all the typical architectural features of that period. It is now a country house hotel. The house is particularly beautiful in the early morning sun, as the stone then shines with a pinkish glow.

Over the stile, turn left and follow the cart track for 200–300 yards, then cross a large meadow surrounded by the woods. At the far side a kissing gate is at the entance to a wood of beech, oak and sycamore. In spring, wild snowdrops carpet the floor of this wood. The path leads through the wood, then comes out into the open for a short period, with wide views of the Conwy river and Conwy Castle and the mountains beyond.

Go downhill, climbing down big steps in the rock, past a spring surrounded by liverwort, and down to a small stream with butterbur and wild garlic growing in great quantities. A brick wall on the left has ivy-leaved toadflax in it and at the end of this brick wall, the stream is crossed by a small concrete bridging slab. Across the little bridge turn right through the kissing gate and walk through the middle of the field to where another gate can clearly be seen in the hedge. Passing this, the path runs up over the hill, then down across another field to the driveway to Bodysgallen Hall. Just before walking onto this driveway (which is more like a lane), turn sharp left and, by an oak tree at the far side of the field, another gate can be seen. Walk up this hill, until the Llandudno to Deganwy road is reached at a point where a finger post marks the path.

Turn left along the pavement and walk along the road for about 100 yards. Cross the road by some houses and walk up the entrance to Bwlch Farm. This leads to the point where the path crossed the driveway previously. Turn left down this path and at the bottom of the short hill, bear left. The small road runs to the left but a path runs up to the right behind the gardens of a row of houses. Follow this, past the Deganwy quarries – a notable geological formation of igneous rock. At the bottom, turn right through a gate and follow the stony path to Deganwy Church and the starting point.

Walk 4   Conwy Mountain and Sychnant Pass

4½ miles (7 km)

Start: Cadnant Park Road or Mountain Road, Conwy,
OS map ref. 777777

This walk goes across the lower slopes of Conwy Mountain, passing
on the way the large Iron Age hill fort of Caer Lleon (or Caer Seion)
and the smaller Alltwen fort. It crosses the Sychnant Pass and goes
through some fine open country behind Conwy. There are some magnificent views of Conwy Bay and Anglesey, as well as of the walled
town of Conwy and its castle. The going is fairly easy on well marked
paths initially and then on country lanes, and can be walked at all
times of the year.

    Dogs need to be kept under control for a large part of the route as
sheep roam freely, both on Conwy Mountain and in the open country
around the Sychnant Pass.

    Bird-watchers will find plenty of interest on this walk, especially
the chance of seeing some birds of open country – stonechats, ravens,
kestrels, linnets and pipits. Botanists will also find plenty of flowers of
open, hill country.

    The start is reached by taking the A55 out of Conwy towards
Bangor. About 200 yards out from the archway through which the
A55 passes, there is a road to the left, which runs across the railway
cutting. This is signposted to Beechwood Court, Conwy Mountain
and Sychnant Pass. Turn sharp right immediately over the bridge
and carry on down Cadnant Park Road. This road curves round to
the left, and on the bend take the lane (Mountain Road) to the right.
This road bears left, to a point where some terraced cottages stand.
Opposite these, there is a car parking space for up to 6 cars, alternatively the car can be parked in Cadnant Park Road, and the starting point put back a few hundred yards down Mountain Road.

    Take the path which runs up the side of the hill past the end of the
terraced cottages. It rises steadily upwards through the gorse and
bracken. After about half a mile, towards the brow of the hill, take a
short diversion to the right onto the top. From here, there is a panoramic view of Conwy Bay, the estuary and the Great Orme and
Llandudno. It is easy to understand how the Great Orme got its name
when seen from this spot, orme being the Norse for sea monster. In the
old days travellers to Ireland by coach had to travel at low tide around
the headland (Penmaenbach) and across the sands which lie below –
a risky business at times.

    Return to the main track and continue walking along it on the
inland side of the ridge. After a further ½ mile, looking up towards the

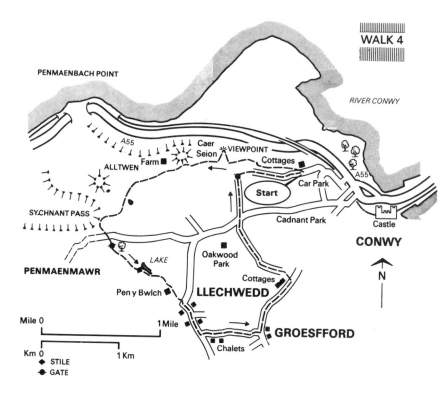

PENMAENBACH POINT

RIVER CONWY

A55
Caer
Seion ✳ VIEWPOINT
Farm ■ ↙ ↓↓↓
ALLTWEN
Cottages ■
A55

SYCHNANT PASS

Start

Car Park

Cadnant Park

Castle

CONWY

N

PENMAENMAWR
LAKE
Oakwood
Park

Cottages ■

Pen y Bwlch ■
LLECHWEDD

GROESFFORD

Mile 0   1 Mile
Km 0   1 Km
◆ STILE
● GATE

Chalets

crest of the ridge the remains of the great hill fort of Caer Lleon can be
seen. The highest point is 808 ft (247 m) above sea level, but the outer
perimeter wall is on almost all the 700 ft contour line. The whole fort
covers about 10½ acres, and was one of the strongest fortified places in
the area. Many of the stones used to build the ramparts are now
thrown down but it is still possible to visualize the layout of the fort.

The main entrance was on the south side facing the path and is still
easily visible. It was so made that a direct assault straight up into the
fort was not possible. There is an outer camp, containing many hut
circle remains, and on the higher ground an inner citadel, similar in
principle to the keep of a castle. All round are the remains of many
ditches and walls for defence. Rounded stones known as 'pot boilers'
can be found, as well as smaller pebble-sized sling stones. The presence of the pot boilers indicates that the people did not use much fire-
resistant pottery, but had to warm water by means of heating these
pot boilers in a fire, then putting the hot stones into the pots. It is likely
that the fort was occupied between two and three thousand years ago.

Continue along the path until it is joined by another, then go
downhill past two ponds, and just past the last of these take the left
fork. This leads down to the head of the Sychnant Pass. This deep

valley was formed by glaciers in the Ice Age. Cross the road here and follow the path directly opposite through a gate. The path leads along beside a small wood on the left. At the end of this wood, bear left slightly to head towards a small lake. Climb the stile over the wall and walk along the grassy track. At the end of the lake the track forks, bear slightly right, keeping to the grassy track. Ahead between two small knolls the path leads onto a stony cart track. Go straight across this cart track and continue alongside a wall, passing a house called Pen-y-Bwlch (Head of the Pass). The track falls away downhill coming out at a lane on a sharp bend. A farm cart decorated with flowers stands here.

Follow the lane to the right, passing over a cattle grid, and, after about $\frac{1}{4}$ mile, take the lane to the left. Berthlwyd Hall holiday chalets are in a field to the right. This narrow lane comes down to Groesffordd (Crossroads) Post Office. Turn left at these crossroads and walk for $\frac{1}{3}$ mile along the lane. A row of cottages is reached and at this point turn left uphill along a track marked 'Unsuitable for Motor Vehicles'. This is a fairly steep climb but eventually comes out onto a metalled lane. Keep along this lane past Oaklands, a huge rambling place. The lane comes out on the Conwy to Sychnant Pass road. Cross straight over, down a cart track towards Conwy mountain. On joining a bridle path running along the valley, turn right and you will come back to the car park by the cottages at Mountain Road and Cadnant Park.

Walk 5　　　Penmaenmawr and the Druids' Circle

10½ miles (19 km)

Start: Penmaenmawr car park, OS map ref. 718764

The country behind Penmaenmawr is the nearest part of the Snowdonia mountains to the sea in the north. The coastal strip at this point is very narrow and the hills rise steeply up behind the town to reach 1000 ft very rapidly. This walk takes in the foothills of some of the higher peaks in Snowdonia as well as providing considerable interest in the large number of prehistoric remains it passes. The going is fairly hard mainly due to having to go up and down the steep escarpment, but underfoot it is easy, with good clearly marked paths and roads to follow, and can be walked throughout the year.

Much of it is through sheep pasture and dogs are definitely not recommended to be taken on this walk.

Apart from the scenery and the prehistoric interest, there is generally plenty of upland bird life to be seen – ravens, curlew, wheatears, pipits, whinchats and possibly choughs.

The start is in the main car park at Penmaenmawr. This car park lies on the landward side of the main A55 coast road and is near to the main cross roads in the centre of the town, which has plenty of cafés and inns.

From the car park turn right, then immediately right again up the road called Y Berlan. At the top of the rise, Y Berlan swings to the left through a housing estate, then turns right up to some slightly older houses. At this point, turn left up a stony cart track. This leads up to Craiglwydd Road, opposite the entrance to Craiglwydd Hall. Half left, across the road, the cart track continues up the hill, passing through a kissing gate, then past a small reservoir. The path leads around the upper edge of this reservoir and crosses to a gate in the wall (OS map ref. 724756). There are some fine views here of Puffin Island and Anglesey.

Through the gate turn left along the wall, past a farm and after about ¼ mile Mountain Road is reached. Turn right up Mountain Road, which is very steep. This road winds up the side of Foel Lus (1180 ft, 360 m), crosses a cattle grid and becomes a stony bridle path. Two stone pillars are reached, which are the start of the Jubilee Walk (Queen Victoria's) around Foel Lus. Take the bridle path to the right here, and follow it for half a mile, to Tyn-y-Ffrith. This hill farm now serves teas and refreshments. Just before reaching Tyn-y-Ffrith take the right path, marked to the Druids' Circle. The track leads across the hills beside a wall, through a couple of gates then past another house, Bryn Derwydd, standing in a clump of trees. The

28

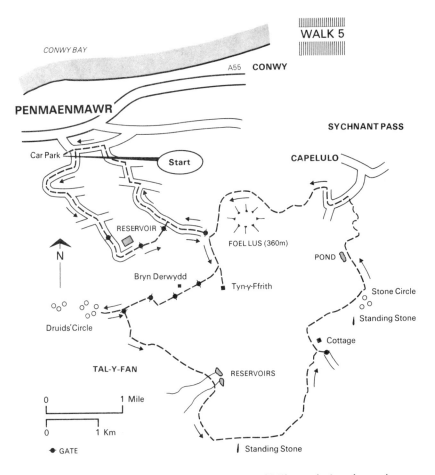

CONWY BAY

A55 CONWY

PENMAENMAWR

SYCHNANT PASS

Car Park

Start

CAPELULO

RESERVOIR

N

FOEL LUS (360m)

POND

Bryn Derwydd

Tyn-y-Ffrith

Stone Circle

Standing Stone

Druids'Circle

Cottage

TAL-Y-FAN

RESERVOIRS

0   1 Mile

0   1 Km

GATE

Standing Stone

country here is very wild, gorse, heather, and bilberry being the main plants, and is the haunt of ravens, whinchats, wheatears, ring ousels, and crows.

At the end of the small belt of Scots pines the path turns sharp right and leads up to a gate in the wall. Pass through and carry on bearing to the left. Ahead in the distance lies the long ridge of Tal-y-Fan (2000 ft, 610 m). On the left the hill rises to 1244 ft (379 m). Follow the wall and this leads to a signpost, the left hand path marked 'Public Footpath', and the right hand 'Druids' Circle'. Take the latter, across the heather and bilberry moor, and very shortly afterwards the stones of the Druids' Circle are seen on the skyline. Follow the path up to the stone circle. This circle is known locally as Meini Hirion (the Long Stones). Writing in the sixteenth century, Sir John Wynne described these stones almost exactly as they are now. The circle is a double one, and is reputed to have been used by the Druids but for what purpose

29

is not now known. A short distance away is another, smaller, less well-preserved circle, and Pennant, writing in 1781, states that there was yet another one close by, but this now seems to have disappeared. Tradition has it that near here a fierce battle was fought between the Romans and the Britons and that these stones were erected to commemorate those who fell.

To the south-west of Meini Hirion is a round-topped hill called Moelfre (OS map ref. 717745) which was also described in the sixteenth century. According to tradition three different coloured stones stood on the top. Each stone represented a woman turned to stone because she winnowed her corn on the top of Moelfre on the Sabbath day. Unfortunately these stones were vandalized and rolled down the hill several centuries ago.

After leaving the Druids' Circle retrace the path to the signpost. From here take the right hand path, marked 'Public Footpath'. This leads past a small radio building and along beside a wall. Keep beside the wall, crossing one or two small streams and bogs. After a short way the wall turns, and at this point continue straight across the heather and bilberry moor. The track becomes very indistinct but by heading towards a small reservoir that can be seen ahead there is no chance of loosing the way (OS map ref. 735744).

On reaching this small reservoir, cross the river and walk around the perimeter fence. Close behind the first reservoir is another one. Cross a second river and walk to the right, away from the two reservoirs and diagonally up the hill from the river. A cart track is reached after about 400 yards and, turning right along it, after about $\frac{1}{4}$ mile another track runs off to the left. This continues to rise up the hill, then levels off. At this point a large standing stone can be seen to the right, set in among several hillocks. The track provides good walking and eventually leads down to an old, deserted, cottage and sheep pens. This is an area where the rare choughs can sometimes be seen, as well as ravens. The choughs are often first noticed by hearing their sharp call, which is quite different from that of the jackdaws and crows.

Take the track which runs behind the cottage (OS map ref. 745747) and follow it across the pasture. Another standing stone can be seen in the middle of the field to the right, and shortly after this a group of stones is passed which look like the remains of a stone circle. Further on a large wooden stile over the wall on the right is reached, and from here three paths radiate out. Take the left hand one which runs through a small valley and past a shallow pond up to a dry stone wall. Keep around to the right, past a small farm and then head downhill, initially between stone walls, then along a narrow path. This drops steeply down into Capelulo, a small village at the bottom of the Sychnant Pass. It was at one time a busy staging post where horses were changed before taking the coaches up the steep pass to Conwy and eastwards. Capelulo has several inns and tea rooms, but if making use of them, return to the point where the path met the metalled road, as the route runs from here to the left up through the woods. These woods in spring are a good place for seeing many woodland birds, especially wood warblers. The path is well surfaced and climbs to the right up onto the mountain side again (OS map ref. 743765). Take the left hand path at the first signpost, then a three way signpost is reached and here the right hand route should be taken, across a small stream. This path eventually joins the Jubilee Walk around Foel Lus. The track circles the hill and comes around to the entrance pillars met with at the beginning of the walk.

From here it is about a mile back to the car park. Walk down Mountain Road to where it meets another road. Turn left, and then right through the lanes and streets of Penmaenmawr, until the car park is reached.

Walk 6   Llanfairfechan

5 miles (8 km)

Start: car park at Llanfairfechan, OS map ref. 692741

The northernmost parts of the mountains of Snowdonia reach the coast at Conwy and run westwards through Penmaenmawr to Llanfairfechan, where the line of hills moves inland, leaving a wider, low-lying, coastal strip. On these hills close to the sea the early inhabitants of the area were very active, and many remains of the Stone, Bronze and Iron Ages can be found. The country behind Llanfairfechan, in particular, provides some fine walking with a rare combination of spectacular views of both the sea and the mountains.

This walk definitely requires good shoes, or boots, and is reasonably hard going, the initial section being uphill and the middle part being across rough, tussocky moorland country, which can be quite tiring to the ankles. Providing good waterproof shoes and clothing are used the walk is suitable for all seasons.

Dogs are not recommended to be brought as, for the majority of the way, the route lies through open hill farming country, and sheep are everywhere.

To reach the start, take the A55 coast road from Conwy to Bangor. At Llanfairfechan, turn inland at the traffic lights – the only set in the town – and drive up through the village, following the signs pointing to Valley Road. A row of houses on the left is reached which are set back off the road and face a green. There is a car park at the end of the green.

From this car park turn right and walk up the hill, for about 100 yards, then bear right over a small bridge. This crosses the Afon Ddu. The road then bears left up beside the river, through the thick woods of oak, mountain ash and blackthorn, eventually emerging into open country. The rocky, hump-shaped hill on the left is Dinas, and was a hill fort in pre-Roman times. On it, there are traces of fourteen huts, 20 to 30 ft in diameter. The floors of these huts would have been roughly paved with stone and there would have been a central pole to support the conical roof.

Passing a picnic place on the left, and a road marked 'private' on the right, keep along a grassy path after going through a swing gate. A small footbridge crosses the Afon Ddu, and the path carries on uphill through an oak wood. It then comes out into the open above the edge of the trees. Bear right and, after 50 yards or so, climb up the side of a grassy hillock, following the course of an old dry stone wall. At a point where a clump of bushes and a broken down signpost is reached, bear left, the path wandering across the pasture to a gap in the stone wall.

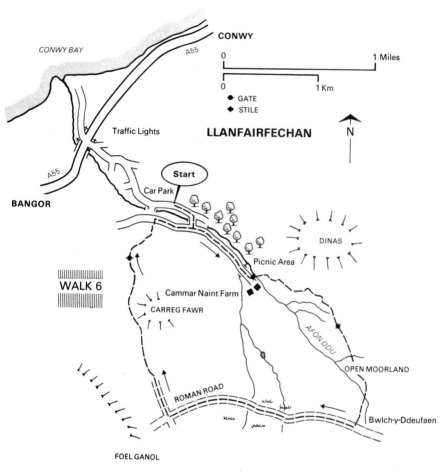

CONWY

CONWY BAY

A55

0   1 Miles

0   1 Km

◆ GATE
◆ STILE

Traffic Lights

LLANFAIRFECHAN   N

A55

Start

Car Park

BANGOR

DINAS

Picnic Area

WALK 6

Cammar Naint Farm

CARREG FAWR

AFON DDU

OPEN MOORLAND

ROMAN ROAD

Bwlch-y-Ddeufaen

FOEL GANOL

This is a very boggy area and stepping-stones have been provided. Beyond this marshy patch the land becomes Ffridd land – rough grazing for sheep, Welsh mountain ponies, and some cattle. Formerly the ground belonged to a farm, now demolished, known as Cadleisia. Records of this farm go back 500 years or more.

The route follows the line of an old cart track across the open moorland, crossing several streams, and heading towards a high stone wall with a gate in it.

Beyond this gate, the mountainside´is common land. Looking around from here there is a marvellous panorama of sea and mountain. Behind, the Menai Straits and Anglesey can be clearly seen, to the left Penmaenmawr, Dinas, and the round topped hill of Moelfre. More to the right the Carneddau range rises up, with Foel Fras at 3090 ft (942 m) being the highest visible from here.

The course of the path is fairly clear over rough ground between clumps of gorse and heather, crossing several small streams, and generally bearing right down into the shallow valley of the Afon Ddu. The large, dry stone, sheep pen that can be seen on the right is of unusual type. The large central section is used by all the farmers to gather their livestock in and each has his own side chamber, so that the sheep can be separated out by their different owners.

Cross the river on the stones and climb up through the bilberries and heather towards the line of pylons which run along the route taken by the Roman road across Bwlch-y-Ddeufaen. These lines take the electricity generated at the Wylfa nuclear power station on Anglesey, to the National Grid. On reaching the Roman road turn right. The road is in good condition and provides a good walking surface, as it winds across the hillsides. There is only one short stretch where the going becomes very soft, but it soon recovers and continues north-westwards, along the slopes of Foel Ganol (1848 ft, 533 m). The power lines follow the course of the road all the way.

After about a mile and a quarter, a meeting of the tracks is reached. The Roman road continues straight, whilst another well-marked track crosses it.

Turn right here and walk down the grassy track, towards Carreg Fawr (1168 ft, 356 m). The rocks of this hill are the same as those used for making the stone axes, providing a hard edge, yet flaking easily. Another multi-chambered sheep pen is passed.

Keep on down the hill, until a kissing gate is reached. From here a good view of Llanfairfechan can be had. Zig-zag down the track until it reaches another gate, skirting Tan Rallt farm. This leads to Terrace Walk and back to the small bridge over the river. Turn left over the bridge and return to the car park.

Walk 7   Roewen and the 'Roman Bridge'

4 miles (6 km)

Start: near the Ty Gwyn Hotel, Roewen, OS map ref. 758720

This walk is along country lanes and grassy tracks all the way. Initially there is a long steep hill to walk up but after the first mile the going becomes much easier. The second half of the walk passes various Neolithic burial chambers, standing stones and cists, as well as following the course of the old Roman road across Bwlch-y-Ddeufaen. The first half is of great interest for its natural history as well as providing outstanding views of the Conwy valley, the Denbigh moors and Snowdonia.

Although the walk is along little used lanes with grass down the middle of them it is necessary to keep dogs under control as the dry stone walls along the route are broken in places and sheep wander freely everywhere. The lanes are very narrow, which means that any traffic is generally travelling fairly slowly, but remember to take care.

Roewen is reached by travelling out of Conwy on the B5106 (Conwy to Llanrwst Road) and after $2\frac{1}{2}$ miles, turning right just past the fifteenth-century Groes Hotel. This road runs for about 2 miles up to Roewen. There is space for parking at the lower end of the village near the Ty Gwyn Hotel. Roewen is a picturesque village, very popular with artists.

Walk up through the village along the main street, passing the Willow Café on the left. The road, which is very narrow, winds up the hill, between dry stone walls, with the Afon Roe on the left cascading down hill. This a particularly attractive river, the river bed being extremely rocky and the hill steep, so there are many cascades and rapids, as well as still pools outside the main flow of water.

This part of the walk is steep, and as the lane climbs up the hill it is interesting to speculate on the effort that has gone into the making of the walls lining the lane. They are made of particularly large boulders, and a lot of energy must have been needed to move them into position, two or three men being needed to lift each one.

As the lane climbs up, the trees lining it become sparser and, on sunny days, lizards can often be seen sunning themselves on the walls. They can move surprisingly fast, so some care is needed to get close to them. Many ferns, and flowers grow here, including pennywort, foxgloves, and ivy-leaved toadflax. Butterflies are also very numerous in the sheltered part of the lane. Redstarts, warblers, and wheatears are common. Further up as the lane rises above the tree level curlews, ravens and buzzards are generally to be seen, with the occasional

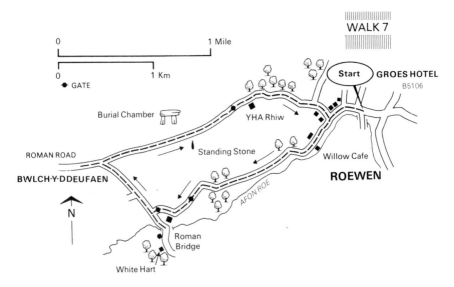

0   1 Mile

0   1 Km
◆ GATE

Start   GROES HOTEL
               B5106

Burial Chamber

YHA Rhiw

ROMAN ROAD

Standing Stone

BWLCH-Y-DDEUFAEN

Willow Cafe

ROEWEN

AFON ROE

N

Roman
Bridge

White Hart

heron, searching the bogs for frogs, and any other likely food.

A gate across the road is reached, pass through it, and on across more open country. To the left is the Conwy valley, whilst half left is Pen-y-Gaer – a large Iron Age hilltop fort. Further on a house is reached which is now derelict – Hafoty Gwyn (White Summer Homestead). This house would have been used during the summer by the farmer; all the family, sheep and cattle moving up from the valley for the summer months. A second gate is reached, and also a T junction. It is worth taking a short diversion to the left down the hill to the little bridge, known as the 'Roman Bridge', which is not in fact Roman but eighteenth century. It is likely, however, that even in Roman times, these narrow lanes were in use by drovers and connected up with the main military marching road across Bwlch-y-Ddeufaen. At the bridge, dippers and grey wagtails can often be seen, and also small trout lie in the deeper pools under the arch. A clump of trees on the hill opposite hides an old building – the White Hart – a relic of the times when this bridge was actually used by drovers bringing their cattle eastwards to the Conwy valley, Llanrwst, and the industrial centres of England.

Retrace the road up the short hill and continue straight along, the road rising gradually. A junction is reached after about half a mile (1 km). To the left is the course of the Roman Road which crossed the Conwy near the Roman fort of Caerhun, and ran through Roewen, up the hill, across Bwlch-y-Ddeufaen and down to the coast at Aber. Until recently a Roman milestone stood beside the road about a mile further along, at the point where the power lines cross over the road.

The route for the walk, however, takes the grassy track to the right.

After half a mile, a well preserved dolmen stands beside the road – known as Maen-y-Bardd (Stone of the Poet). This consists of a capstone and four upright stones, still in position. About 50 yards to the east lie the remains of a stone cist (or stonechest), measuring about 10 ft long by 4 ft. The cist was a later form of burial than the dolmen. Slightly up the hillside to the west are two stones which appear to be part of a stone circle; also nearby to the west and hidden by the wall is a large standing stone – Maen Hir (Long Stone). This whole area, therefore, was actively used by Neolithic man about 3000–4000 years ago. The reasons for siting these various dolmens, cists and standing stones in these positions is the subject of a great deal of interest nowadays – some suggesting that standing stones, particularly, were way markers, whilst others think they may have been indicators of hidden earth forces, which give out fields of power at present undetected. Certainly there is ample scope in this area to test out many of these theories.

A gate is reached. Go downhill, past the Youth Hostel at Rhiw Farm. This hill is a very steep one and needs almost as much effort going down as walking up it. Roewen is finally reached. Turn left to return to the car.

Walk 8   Llanbedr-y-Cennin and Pen-y-Gaer

4 miles (6 km)

Start: Olde Bull Inn, Llanbedr-y-Cennin, OS map ref. 761695

Like the previous one, this walk is along country lanes and up grassy tracks, and provides beautiful views of the Conwy Valley and the hills to the east, and, later, of Snowdonia. Although short in distance, parts are fairly steep, so allow plenty of time to complete the round. Initially through wooded country on the side of the Conwy Valley, it comes out onto open land above Llanbedr-y-Cennin, and passes by Pen-y-Gaer – an internationally famous Iron Age hill fort.

The walk passes through open sheep grazing country, so dogs must be kept under control for long stretches of the route.

Llanbedr-y-Cennin is reached by driving along the B5106 road from Conwy to Llanrwst and turning up the hill past the Y Bedol (Horseshoe) Inn in Tal-y-Bont. This is 6 miles from both Conwy and Llanrwst. Cars can be parked beside the road up the hill leading to the Olde Bull Inn, or permission to use the Inn car park must be obtained from the landlord.

Llanbedr-y-Cennin is an old village, notable for the Holy Well, Ffynon Bedr, which was a place for pilgrims in the Middle Ages. The Olde Bull Inn and Church House opposite were in those days used as resting houses for the pilgrims, but now the Olde Bull Inn is a very pleasant pub and Church House is a privately owned residence. The well is not open to the public. Llanbedr-y-Cennin in the more modern times of the eighteenth and nineteenth centuries was also noted for its annual horse fair.

Starting at the Olde Bull Inn, walk up the hill and take the second lane on the left, this being about $\frac{1}{4}$ mile from the Inn. Walking along this lane, a farm is reached. Take the track which runs up to the right of this farm. Follow this track up across the hillside, through wooded country. Around here, mixed sheep and cattle farming is practised, Welsh Blacks being particularly numerous. This breed of cattle is adapted for living on the damper hillsides of Wales and is a dual purpose breed being used for both dairy and meat production. The Welsh Blacks have larger horns than other breeds of cattle likely to be seen around this part of Wales – Friesians, Charolais, Ayrshires and Shorthorns. The wooded countryside is good for seeing sparrow hawks, jays, green and great spotted woodpeckers and a variety of smaller woodland birds – bullfinches, in particular, seem to be common here. Barn owls can also be fairly often seen, especially on a dull autumn or spring evening or at dusk in the summer. The notably

38

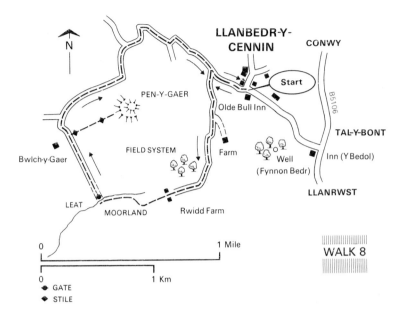

WALK 8

0   1 Mile

0   1 Km

● GATE
● STILE

large number of old derelict cottages and farm buildings here are, no doubt, an attraction for the owls.

The track continues to curve round the hill between stone walls. Rwidd Farm is reached; it is no longer lived in, although the outbuildings are still used for livestock. Pass straight through into the open country along the narrow track between the walls. At the end of these walls, keep along this track, until a service road running alongside a Water Authority leat is reached. Turn left along this service road and walk for about $\frac{1}{4}$ mile, then turn right and cross a Welsh National Water Development Authority's bridge, walking towards a farm road that is visible straight ahead running over the hill.

Climb the gate and carry on along this farm road. Pen-y-Gaer is $\frac{1}{4}$ mile away on the right. A stile over the wall on the right leads onto a path through the heather running up to another stile and then to Pen-y-Gaer (Fort on the Top). This fort would have been occupied just before or at about the time of Julius Caesar (100 BC–50 BC), and possibly earlier. It is unique in England and Wales in that it was particularly heavily fortified, mainly on the slopes facing the path across from the stile, and around to the right. The only other similar fortifications are found in Scotland and on the Aran Islands in Ireland. At the top a great rubble wall, still 5 ft high, guards an inner stronghold, but to reach this final wall several hazards had to be overcome. These can best be seen round to the right hand side of the fort. Firstly there was a small ditch followed by a long slope, which would take the impetus out of the first charge of any attackers, the slope

39

being deliberately littered with boulders to make a concerted rush difficult. A ditch, followed by a further rampart would have added to the difficulties of an assault party. A second ditch after the rampart in which 'chevaux de frise' were placed would have meant that any group would be broken up and stoned by the defenders. The 'chevaux de frise' can still be seen in parts – pointed stones about 1–3 ft high stuck in the ground in great numbers. It should be remembered that 2000 years ago the ditches were deeper and had much steeper sides. Inside the fortifications are the remains of several hut circles.

After seeing Pen-y-Gaer it is best to return to the stile and carry on along the farm road to the right. This passes downhill, meeting a lane coming from the left after about half a mile. Continue down the hill, with good views of the Conwy valley until the Olde Bull is reached.

Walk 9   Maenan School and the Conwy Valley

3½ miles (5 km)

Start: Maenan School, OS map ref. 795665

Although outside the boundaries of the National Park and on the eastern side of the river Conwy, the area covered by this walk provides impressive views of the Conwy valley, Gwydyr Forest, and the hills of Snowdonia rising up behind. It is a pleasant walk through sunken lanes, very different in character from those across the valley, and this illustrates very well the sharp difference between the countryside on the older Ordovician rocks of the western bank of the Conwy and that on the younger Silurian rocks found on this eastern side.

Most of the walk is on firm ground – forest tracks and cart tracks, as well as lanes – and is especially pleasant in the winter.

Dogs can be taken, as no livestock should be met with.

The starting point is at Maenan School. This is best reached by taking the road marked to Llandoget, opposite the old cinema car park in Llanrwst. After about 400 yards the road to Llandoget turns right, the Maenan School road goes left. Maenan School is about 2½ miles up this road, turning right, then immediately left and left again. The school is a typical little country schoolhouse, surprisingly set by itself in a heavily wooded area.

Park by the school and walk through the gate into a Forestry Commission plantation. There is a signpost marked 'Cadair Ifan Goch'. Walk down the forest ride, up a steep incline and across a clearing. This undisturbed piece of woodland is a good place to catch a glimpse of a fox and, on sunny summer days, many butterflies can be seen about the forest ride – orange tips, speckled woods, tortoiseshells, and peacocks. Keep straight on across the clearing, bearing slightly right through the remains of an old gateway. The wood here is of birch, spruce, and mountain ash.

A fork in the path is reached. The left hand path goes to a notable view point Cadair Ifan Goch. From here, there is a magnificent view along the Conwy Valley and westwards across to Snowdonia. Cadair Ifan Goch means Seat of Red Ifan and this rocky hill was reputed to be the stronghold of this early Welsh Chieftain. Caer Oleu is another Iron Age hill fort, now hidden in the woods on the way to Cadair Ifan Goch. It is a smaller fort than Caerhun mentioned in Walk 4, or Pen-y-Gaer described in Walk 7, which is virtually just across the valley from Caer Oleu. Caer Oleu means Beacon Rock or Bright Rock.

Retrace the path to where the track forked and take the right hand path, initially up the hillside, then dropping down again. An iron gate

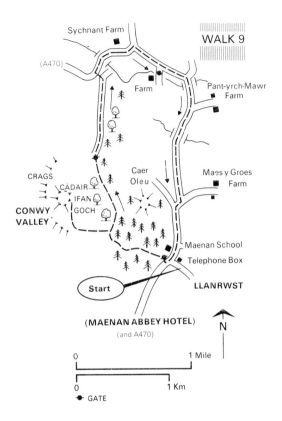

Sychnant Farm

(A470)

Farm

Pant-yrch-Mawr
Farm

Caer
Oleu

CRAGS

Maes y Groes
Farm

CADAIR
IFAN
GOCH

CONWY
VALLEY

Maenan School

Telephone Box

Start

LLANRWST

(MAENAN ABBEY HOTEL)

(and A470)

N

0   1 Mile

0   1 Km

GATE

is reached and on going through the gateway a farm track leads on past several small farms and cottages (OS map ref. 788674). This track leads to a driveway which swings downhill onto a lane. Turn right here and follow the lane. This climbs steeply for a short way, past the entrance to a house called Sychnant. At the next road junction turn right past a farm.

About 200 yards further on a farm entrance is reached. There is, in fact, a public right of way as marked on the Ordnance Survey maps which goes along this entrance and across the farm land, but, through lack of use, and the difficulty for the farmer of keeping the path clear the exact route is now no longer obvious. This section illustrates very well the decline of footpaths in this whole area. Many landowners maintain that the paths were originally declared public to allow farm workers, miners, etc. to get to work, or to Church, and were not intended for use by large numbers of the general public, consequently they are disinclined to keep the paths cleared. Certainly there is no doubt that many of the public rights of way marked on the Ordnance Maps, by lack of usage, are no longer easily traceable on the ground.

42

In view of this problem, for this walk, continue past the farm entrance up the lane to the next T junction, then turn right. Follow this lane, between high hazel hedges, past Maes-y-Groes farm, and back to Maenan School.

It is interesting to note that this part of the country looks far more prosperous and fertile than the land just across the valley in Snowdonia, again an indication of the difference in soil and underlying rock formations.

Walk 10   Llanrwst and Trefriw

$3\frac{1}{2}$ miles (5 km)

Start: Llanrwst station, OS map ref. 795623

This walk is on the flat all the way and is suitable for all times of the year. The route goes along the flood wall of the river Conwy to the large village of Trefriw, then back to Llanrwst. The meadows alongside the river are all sheep pastures, so dogs must be kept under control for the first half of the walk. At Trefriw, at one time a thriving commercial centre, there are the old established woollen mills, which are still very active. Welsh tweed is woven here and during normal working hours people can visit the mill and see the complete production process from the grading and carding of the oiled wool to the spinning and doubling, dyeing, and finally weaving. No charge is made to do this. There is, also, a very large display of woollen goods on sale on the ground floor of the newly built, stone, mill house. About a mile and half northwards out of the village lie Trefriw spa and caves. This small spa was a great attraction in Victorian times for drinking and bathing in the separate springs of iron and sulphur waters. Nowadays the small caves where the springs flow are open to visitors.

The walk starts at Llanrwst, an ancient market town in the Conwy Valley, lying about 15 miles south of Llandudno and about 4 miles north of Betws-y-Coed on the A470 road. It has an interesting church with a family chapel next to it. The town was devastated in the Wars of the Roses and in the earlier Welsh rebellions of Owain Glyndwr, and was also involved in the Civil War. It has a fine bridge over the river built in 1634, which is reputed to have been designed by Inigo Jones. For several hundred years this was the only road bridge crossing the River Conwy below Betws-y-Coed, until Telford built the suspension bridge at Conwy in 1826.

Park in the station car park, the station lying to the north of the town. Take the tarmac road leading out of the car park towards the river. Cross the suspension footbridge known as Gower's bridge, and on the far bank turn right over a stile to reach the path which goes alongside the river on top of the flood wall. This wall follows the course of the river for about $1\frac{1}{2}$ miles, coming eventually to a channel entering the river on a bend. Turn left alongside this stream and walk into Trefriw.

The water meadows are always full of bird life. In the summer, swallows, sand martins, grey and pied wagtails and herons are all likely to be seen. In spring and autumn it may be possible to see kingfishers on the river, as well as to flush snipe up from boggy

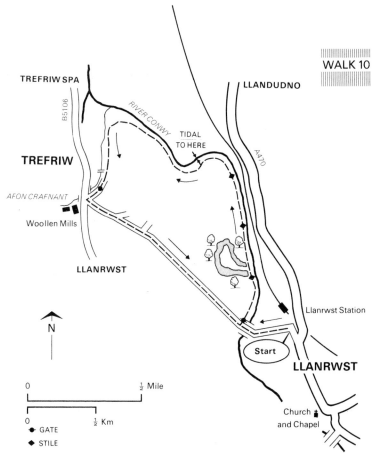

TREFRIW SPA

LLANDUDNO

B5106

RIVER CONWY

TIDAL TO HERE

TREFRIW

A470

AFON CRAFNANT

Woollen Mills

LLANRWST

N

Llanrwst Station

Start

LLANRWST

0   ½ Mile

0   ½ Km
◆ GATE
◆ STILE

Church and Chapel

patches beside the walls. Kestrels are also often seen here.

Waterside plants are prolific along the whole stretch and a plant identification book is well worth taking.

The woollen mills are opposite the point where the path reaches the main road in Trefriw. To reach the spa and caves turn right and walk along the road for an extra $1\frac{1}{2}$ miles (3 miles there and back).

During the last century, and earlier, Trefriw was the limit for river boats coming down from Conwy and it was a centre for exporting timber and lead ore from mines in the hills behind. The ore was dragged on sledges down through the woods to the river. River steamer trips also brought people to the spa. Nowadays no boats of this size come up as far as Trefriw – the river clearly having become much shallower in these reaches.

To return to Llanrwst, take the road running down towards Llanrwst from opposite the woollen mills. This goes back to Gower's bridge and the Llanrwst station car park.

Walk 11   Llyn Geirionydd and Llyn Crafnant

6 miles (10 km)

Start: Llyn Geirionydd car park, OS map ref. 763604

Walks 11 to 15 are all based on Gwydyr Forest. This large forest, covering in all about 20,000 acres (8000 hectares) and first planted in 1921, is located around Betws-y-Coed, Llanrwst, and Penmachno. The whole area is extensively planted with a variety of conifers – Sitka spruce, Japanese larch, Norway spruce, lodgepole pine, Douglas fir and Scots pine amongst others, each species being chosen for its ability to grow in the soil and weather conditions prevailing in particular parts of the area. About nine per cent of the timber in the forest is hardwood, which helps to break up the monotony of large plantations of conifers. This, added to the rocky nature of the country, and the large open areas with far distant views, makes Gwydyr Forest particularly enjoyable for walking in at all times of the year.

The first of this group of walks goes through a good variety of country as well as being an excellent walk through the northernmost edge of Gwydyr Forest and around the two lakes. It is moderately easy going, but in places goes across soft ground, so good shoes are essential. Since the walk is mainly through Forestry Commission land, dogs can roam freely without fear of disturbing livestock.

The hill between Llyn (Lake) Geirionydd and Llyn Crafnant rises to 1200 ft (366 m) at its highest point. The Forestry Commission road, however, takes a fairly easy way up over the hill. Llyn Geirionydd's catchment area for water lies on a vein of rock rich in lead, consequently the water in the lake has a high lead content and no fish can survive in it. The water in Llyn Geirionydd is always very clear, due to the scarcity of water plants growing in it, for the lead affects their growth too. On the other hand, Llyn Crafnant, at the other side of the hill, does not have this characteristic and trout fishing is good. The ridge separating the two lakes is the dividing line of the lead rich strata. Llyn Geirionydd is used for water skiing, sailing and canoeing, whilst Llyn Crafnant is used for fishing. This whole northern section of Gwydyr Forest, lying behind Trefriw and to the north of Betws-y-Coed is full of old lead mine workings. It is advisable not to stray off the paths as, whilst the old shafts are mostly wired off, there is always a chance of coming across a hidden one.

Llyn Geirionydd has a car park and picnic site at its southern end. It is reached by driving over narrow roads either out of Trefriw where Llyn Geirionydd is signposted, (there are six gates to pass on this

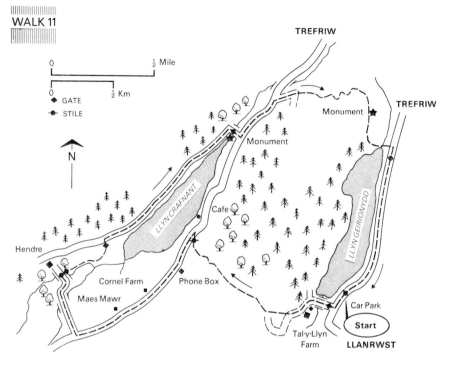

route) or by taking the road at Gwydyr Castle, Llanrwst, signposted to Nant B.H. and then, after 3 miles, turning right just past a derelict lead mine.

From the car park, turn left and walk down past the picnic site to the dinghy park. Turn right past the dinghy park and up the hill. Take the left hand road past the back of the old farm, Tal-y-Llyn (End of the Lake), the road rising steadily up through the edge of the forest. After about 150 yards, a footpath goes to the right off the Forestry Commission road. This road winds round and the footpath cuts across it again. Keep on the path, which is soft in places, cross another Forestry Commission road and pass through a mature spruce plantation. The path climbs fairly steeply here, eventually reaching another Forestry Commission road at a bend. Turn onto this road to the left, then after about 50 yards take the footpath upwards which leads to the crest of the hill. This passes through a gap in a low stone wall and at this point Llyn Crafnant comes into view, with the mountains of the Carneddau range beyond.

Follow the path downwards towards Llyn Crafnant. Cross a stile onto the lakeside road, near to the Cyn Clwyd café, which is open during the summer. The route, however, goes to the left along the lakeside road, passing a telephone box. This is painted grey-green, as are all telephone boxes in the National Park, to blend in with the landscape. Cornel Farm is reached and further on Maes Mawr (Big Field) farm. About $\frac{1}{4}$ mile beyond Maes Mawr turn right through a gate, onto a track leading to Hendre (Winter Dwelling) which is a café. This part of the route has one or two summer houses tucked away in the woods, looking out along the length of the Llyn Crafnant. Just before reaching the gate to Hendre, take the path to the right, over a stile. The path runs across a meadow alongside a stream for several hundred yards, then it goes towards the forestry plantation, past a ruined cottage. This meadow is rich in plants which prefer wet ground. Cross the stile into the plantation and follow the Forestry Commission road to the right, which runs along beside the lake. Walk the length of the lake, climbing over a gate at the far end. A small monument stands here, commemorating the gift of the lake to the people of Trefriw in the late nineteenth century.

The road from Trefriw passes by here. Walk down it to the left, alongside the Afon Crafnant. This is a very lovely valley in the warmth of summer, full of woodland birds, waterside and hill flowers, and butterflies. About $\frac{1}{4}$ mile downhill, bear to the right off the road, over a stile onto a Forestry Commission road. There is a Forestry Commission notice here saying 'Crafnant View Walk'. This road leads upwards and, at the first hairpin bend, leave the road and carry straight on, over the stile and past the old slate tips and quarry workings. The path winds its way in a rather zig-zag fashion along the hillside. Another lead mine used to be worked here – optimistically called the Klondyke mine! The old mine buildings in the valley far below are the best preserved of any of the local mines.

The path passes a wood, then divides. Take the right hand fork up a short, steep, hill. Llyn Geirionydd comes into view at the top of this hill. Walk to a monument at the near end of the lake. From here take the farm track which runs from a house in the woods, to the lakeside road. Walk back beside the lake through the two gates, to the car park at the far end of the lake. Geirionydd being almost devoid of water life does not have many birds on it, but there is a colony of black-headed gulls nesting on the rocks at the north-eastern end of the lake, and, in the summer, sandpipers can be seen at the lakeside. Llyn Crafnant often has duck on it, especially mallard and mergansers, whilst, in winter, rarer water birds may be seen there, such as grebes and wild swans.

Sheep farming is the main occupation of
those living in the mountains of Snowdonia

The old drovers' road running down to Tremadoc Bay
with the Lleyn peninsula in the far distance

Aberglaslyn Pass

View over Snowdon across Llyn Padarn

Walk 12

4½ miles (7 km)

Llyn Glangors and
Nant Bwlch-yr-haiarn

Start: Bwlch-yr-haiarn car park near Llyn Sarnau, OS map ref. 778592

This part of Gwydyr Forest is particularly beautiful, in that it is interspersed with wide open areas of moorland and upland hill pasture, known as the Nant. There are also several lead mines, now derelict, in the area and the whole of the plateau is riddled with mine tunnels and old shafts. Lead mining had its heyday in the eighteenth and nineteenth centuries, although the Parc mine, near to Llanrwst, was operated for a short while in the 1950s. The walk follows a circular route from Llyn Sarnau (Llyn y Sarnau on the Ordnance Survey map) through the forest, and is initially along a narrow road, then over Forestry Commission roads. There are fine views of the mountains from many different points along the way, and Llyn Glangors, if not being used by fishermen, often has duck on it. Dogs are able to roam freely, as being over Forestry Commission ground there should be no sheep loose.

The walk starts at Llyn Sarnau where there is a large car parking area just beside the road. This narrow, hilly, road runs from Gwydyr Castle, near Llanrwst, (OS map ref. 794611) to Ty Hyll (the Ugly House) (OS map ref. 755575) on the A5. Llyn Sarnau is about half way between these two places. It is recommended that the approach is made from the Gwydyr Castle end, as the turning off the A5 at the Ugly House onto this small road is on a sharp bend and the turn can be difficult and dangerous, especially if unfamiliar with the route. Llyn Sarnau is now dried up but fills after prolonged heavy rain. The Field Centre near to Llyn Sarnau is run by Clwyd County Council, and the lead mine workings just behind it are part of the Llanrwst mine.

On leaving the car take the road to the left away from the Field Centre, past some old cottages, and up a short hill, until on the right an entrance to the forest is reached. This is marked 'Llyn Glangors Walk'. Go round the gate and onto the Forestry Commission road. At the first junction go right. A deep mine shaft is just here. It is well fenced in, but take care. The road goes through a stand of Scots firs. On the hillside here are the remains of various buildings and walls, remnants of a time when all this area was farmed, before being given over to forestry. Crossbills and lesser redpolls are frequently to be seen in this section, both species having increased in recent years with the increase of pine forest, much of which is now just reaching maturity.

49

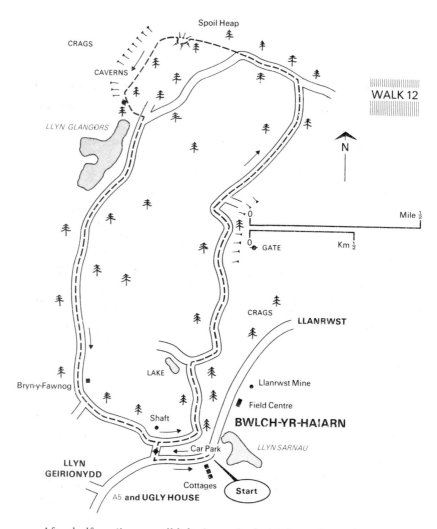

CRAGS

Spoil Heap

CAVERNS

LLYN GLANGORS

N

Mile ½

GATE

Km ½

CRAGS

LLANRWST

Llanrwst Mine

Field Centre

BWLCH-YR-HAIARN

LAKE

Bryn-y-Fawnog

Shaft

LLYN SARNAU

Car Park

LLYN
GEIRIONYDD

Cottages

Start

A5 and UGLY HOUSE

After half a mile, a small lake is reached; this is used as a drinking supply reservoir. Take the right fork at the T junction. There is a notice here, 'Chapel Walk', and, after a further ¼ mile, another similar notice on the right. A small diversion through the trees to the cliff edge provides a fine view of the valley and forest. Take care near the very steep cliffs.

Returning to the road, carry on. The trees here are thicker and younger – about 15–20 years old, they have not yet been thinned. Birdlife in this age of densely planted coniferous wood is limited – goldcrests, willow warblers (in the summer), jays, coal tits and wrens – are generally the only species seen, or, more often, heard. The road runs downhill slightly and curves to the right. A mine spoil heap from the Hafna mine is crossed, as is a track running straight up and down the hill. Keep on the road past a footpath sign on the right. A further T junction is reached. Keep to the right, and at the next junction go left. This is another area of more mature trees, much favoured by crossbills, siskins and redpolls. Views across the open country can be had here. At a long U bend, about $\frac{1}{4}$ mile further on, a footpath sign to the right through the trees is found. This path is marked by white bands on the trees and passes the remains of an old cottage, then reaching a slate quarry spoil heap. Cross the small stream and clamber up the side of the spoil heap, following the line of the path, which is quite clear. A more pronounced path is reached, running uphill to the left – follow this. On the right hand side there are high crags, and just beneath these crags beyond where the path was met, there are some very large caverns, which are impressive to see, the path to the entrance being through a narrow cleft in two rocks. Care should be taken in clambering about in these caverns, although they contain no hidden shafts, and they should not be dangerous to visit. Further up the hill the footpath reaches a fence and a small gate; do not go through the gate but bear left, keeping as near as possible to the fence. After about 100 yards a Forestry Commission road is reached. Turn right and walk past Llyn Glangors. This is a good fishing lake and, when not being fished, several species of duck can usually be seen on it, especially mallard and red breasted merganser. Herons, also, know about the fish!

The road takes a long downhill drop to Bryn-y-Fawnog (Hill of Peat), a solitary house looking out across the hills to the south. On the right there are fine views of Cwm Eigiau, and some very rugged peaks rising to nearly 3000 ft. Black cock (or black grouse) can sometimes be seen on this stretch, Gwydyr Forest being a stronghold for this species. Keep straight on past the next junction and after a short while turn right to the gate which was passed at the start of the walk. On the public road, turn left and walk back to the car park at Llyn Sarnau.

Walk 13   Llyn Sarnau, Llyn Parc and Diosgydd

5 miles (8 km)

Start: Bwlch-yr-haiarn car park near Llyn Sarnau,
OS map ref. 778592

This walk provides a good variety of terrain, from Forestry Commission roads to tracks through the woods and also some steep footpaths. The length is given as 5 miles but the going is fairly hilly and the walk is quite energetic, so allow plenty of time. It is suitable for all times of the year.

The route provides some fine views not only of Nant Bwlch-yr-haiarn but also of the Llugwy valley, through which runs Telford's London to Holyhead road – the A5. Several ruined lead mines are passed, also Llyn Parc and several smaller lakes. Since the walk is mostly over Forestry Commission ground, dogs are free to roam without fear of worrying livestock.

It is important to keep precisely to the route instructions as, on this walk particularly, it is very easy to become lost in the maze of roads criss-crossing the forest. More OS map references than usual are given to help the walker keep on course.

The start is from the large car parking space close to Llyn Sarnau (or Llyn y Sarnau) and the same as for walk 12. This place is called Bwlch-yr-haiarn. It is reached by taking the small road from Gwydyr Castle to Ty Hyll (the Ugly House) on the A5. The latter turning point off the A5 is on a sharp bend on the busy A5 and it is recommended to approach the start from the Gwydyr Castle side.

Keeping the modern field centre on the left, and Llyn Sarnau on the right walk up the Forestry Commission road, passing around a locked gate across the road. On the left, just behind the Field Centre stands the chimney and remains of the Llanrwst lead mine. Llyn Sarnau is very shallow and in dry weather parts of it dry out completely. It has, in fact, a 'leak' and water seeps away through a fault in the rocks.

The road climbs gently, with a group of fields on the right, passing on the left a small white cottage, now used as an outdoor activities centre. Over the brow of the hill the road becomes a grassy track and then joins another road (OS map ref. 785585). Bear to the left along this road. A farmstead on the right is reached, then a T junction, with a small reedy lake on the left. Take the right hand road. In the summer this little lake is full of insects, particularly some fine specimens of dragonflies. Butterflies of various species are very common here and also tree pipits, pied wagtails and sedge warblers are all plentiful at this spot.

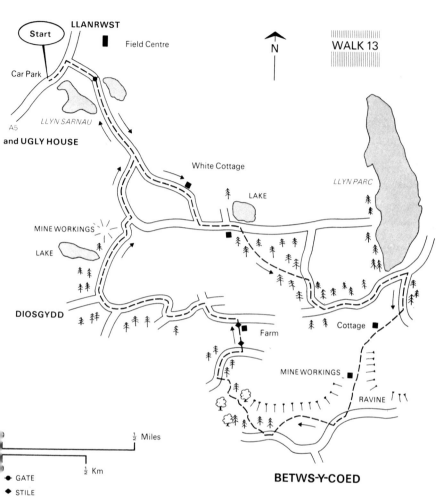

LLANRWST

Start

Field Centre

Car Park

N

A5

LLYN SARNAU

and UGLY HOUSE

White Cottage

LAKE

LLYN PARC

MINE WORKINGS

LAKE

DIOSGYDD

Farm

Cottage

MINE WORKINGS

RAVINE

½ Miles

½ Km

BETWS-Y-COED

◆ GATE

◆ STILE

Shortly after leaving the lake, take a path to the right through the trees. The trees have yellow markers and by following these through the plantation there is no problem in keeping to the route. At the next Forestry Commission road (OS map ref. 790585) turn right, then, on reaching a T junction, left. This road emerges into open ground, with another farmstead to the right. On the left can be seen Llyn Parc (OS map ref. 794584).

Llyn Parc is a long narrow lake and is like Llyn Geirionydd in Walk 11, in that the natural pollution by the lead ore in the rocks around the lake means that no fish live in it. Looking up the lake, on the right, there is an area of high country known as Gwydyr High Park, which is surrounded completely by a stone wall, built by French prisoners in

53

Napoleonic times as an enclosed deer park. At the end of Llyn Parc, turn right, and follow the road down beside the open field.

After a very short distance a path runs across to the right. The ravine ahead is quite spectacular and is also the site of another lead mine – Aber Llyn. Remains of the old machinery can be seen, and this mine gives a particularly good idea of the problems involved in getting the ore down to a place where it could be transported to the smelter.

Keep on past the old mine workings, and walk down the path which leads along the edge of the wooded gorge. A river runs downhill here also, and the path after a while breaks away from this stream, eventually coming into the open with a view of the A5 below. After about 200 yards, just before a notice saying 'Cyrau Walk', bear right uphill. This path runs through a section of cleared woodland and at intervals yellow marking paint on rocks and trees can be seen. Keep on this main path which winds along the side of the hill above Betws-y-Coed, gradually descending into the valley of the Afon Llugwy. This path eventually reaches a stony track, beside another notice for Cyrau Walk.

Turn right up this stony path, past a series of pink marking signs. The going here is fairly steep, but there are some fine views of the mountains behind Capel Curig. The path comes out into an open area and joins a Forestry Commission road. There is a farm, Pen-yr-Allt, on the left, standing in open ground (OS map ref. 785575). Jays, redstarts and buzzards are common around this part of the woods. This is also an area where polecats are found regularly.

Following the Forestry Commission road bear round to the right and a deserted farmhouse comes into view on the left. There is a stile over the wall and a track running across the fields to this farmhouse. Climb a second stile and turn left on the Forestry Commission road. Keep on this road and do *not* follow the orange markers to the right.

At the next road junction go left, first of all downhill, then uphill. Pass a gate and stile, and continue until a notice saying 'Diosgydd Uchaf' is reached. Follow the direction marked by this sign and, at the next sign to Diosgydd Uchaf pointing to the left, keep straight on (OS map ref. 776579). The trees here are fairly large and about thirty to forty years old. The more open canopy allows a greater variety of wild life to thrive, siskins and lesser redpolls can often be seen in this part of the forest.

The Forestry Commission road passes an open space in the woods on the left. There is a small lake just here which, like Llyn Sarnau, is very shallow and mostly reed covered. Just past this open space more mine workings are found – outlying diggings of the Cyffty mine. The road then curves to the left, rising up past these workings. Good views can be had of the hills above Llyn Cowlyd from here. On joining another road, go left and this, after $\frac{1}{4}$ mile will come to Llyn Sarnau and the car parking area.

Walk 14

Betws-y-Coed and Llyn Elsi

$4\frac{1}{2}$ miles (7 km)

Start: Betws-y-Coed station car park, OS map ref. 795565

Like the previous three walks this is through Gwydyr Forest, but it takes in the country to the south of Betws-y-Coed and covers the area between the Llugwy and Lledr valleys. The route is steep to start with, as the path rises up from Betws-y-Coed onto the broad ridge of high country between the two valleys. Once on the top, the going is fairly easy. Being on Forestry Commission land, no livestock should be about and dogs can safely roam. It is suitable for all times of the year. As with all the other walks in Gwydyr, it is important to follow the directions concerning Forestry Commission roads carefully.

The start is in Betws-y-Coed, itself, at the car park close to the station, which is just off the main A5 London to Holyhead road.

From the car park, walk across the field along the public path. This comes to the A5 just opposite the parish church. In fact, Betws-y-Coed means Church in the Wood. Cross the main road and take the road which runs up just past the church on the right. Go past a gate and sign marked 'Church Walk'. Do not take this path, but follow the road up through the woods. This part of the walk is fairly steep, as the road winds up the hill. These oak woods in early summer are full of warblers, especially wood warblers, blackcaps, and garden warblers, and also pied flycatchers. The former are elusive as they move about in the tree tops, but the flycatchers are generally quite approachable and easy to watch. Redstarts can be seen here, also.

A purple marker and bench is reached, and further on another bench. The road swings to the right, past a small stream rushing down the hillside. Keep on the main track past a path running off to the right. Shortly after this the track emerges into open country out of the woods, bearing right along the edge of the escarpment. The woods change at this point from oak and broad leaved trees to evergreens and coniferous species. It is interesting to note the change in bird life from one wood to the other.

Ignore a path, marked with green, going downwards to the left, and keep straight on, bearing to the right at the next fork in the Forestry Commission road. A ruined cottage almost overgrown with ivy and creepers stands on the right, go past it and further on, at the next junction, turn left. This road has a Forestry Commission road sign marked '40' beside it. The woods change to more mature firs, which have been thinned out and consequently the bird life changes again. This time not so much in species as in numbers.

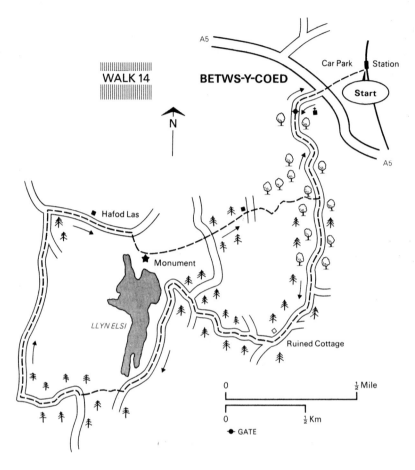

WALK 14

BETWS-Y-COED

A5

Car Park Station

Start

A5

N

Hafod Las

Monument

LLYN ELSI

Ruined Cottage

0   ½ Mile

0   ½ Km

◆ GATE

Keep straight on, ignoring a left hand fork marked '40' and go on past a red marker. At the next T junction go left; the road leads into open country, with views of the Moelwyns and Llyn Elsi ahead. Walk down the Forestry road to the lakeside and then head towards the southern end of the lake. Fish are plentiful in this lake and the fishing is good, consequently when the fishermen are not about there is always the chance to see fish-eating water birds: herons, mergansers, kingfishers and grebes. This open country attracts many tree pipits and cuckoos in the summer – the cuckoos feed on the big woolly caterpillars found amongst the heather and also make use of the meadow pipits nests for laying their eggs in. In winter, rarer over-wintering wild fowl may be seen.

At the southern end of Llyn Elsi is a small dam. The road curves away from the lake here, going downhill, then it swings around the end of the lake (OS map ref. 784548). On this bend, turn right onto a footpath which goes through the trees and appears to be heading back towards the dam at the end of the lake. This leads through several clearings in the wood. The going can be quite soft here especially in spring and autumn or after rain. The path climbs uphill, wending its way between the rocks, then it goes through a plantation of young trees about fifteen to twenty years old, finally running downhill to meet a forest road.

Turn right along this road. Across the open country there are fine views of Moel Siabod, and the other mountains of Snowdonia, best identified by the use of map and compass. Moel Siabod, because of its characteristic whale back shape, is one of the most prominent mountains in the whole area, although not amongst the highest. It rises to 2860 ft (872 m). This stretch of open country with gorse and heather is a haunt of stonechats, and black grouse also seem to favour this part of the forest. The road runs northwards for about $\frac{3}{4}$ mile through young conifer plantations. Llyn Elsi can be seen on the right hand side.

At the next T junction turn left, downhill, through patches of scrub, birch, and rocky outcrops, interspersed with Scots pine – one of the few native conifers to be found here. Norway spruce, Sitka spruce, lodgepole pine, and Japanese larch are all foreign introductions of the Forestry Commission. At the bottom of the hill, turn right onto a road marked '66'.

There is a farmstead, Hafod Las (Blue Summer Dwelling) on the left. A short way further on a small monument can be seen on the right. This stands at the northern end of Llyn Elsi. Take the footpath through the heather which runs up to this monument. At the top of the small hill there is a fine view down the length of Llyn Elsi. From this point the path is marked by blue markers. Following these, the path crosses a Forest road and comes on through the woods. Another Forest road is reached, cross this and keep on downhill, past a ruined cottage. The path then runs in a series of zig-zags steeply downwards through a mixed wood of oak, sycamore, and elm, eventually meeting the road taken at the start of the walk. Turn downhill until the church is reached. Betws-y-Coed has plenty of cafés, pubs and hotels to suit all tastes, mostly up the A5 to the left from here.

57

Walk 15

7½ miles (12 km)

Penmachno and
Bishop Morgan's House

Start: Penmachno, OS map ref. 790505

This is one of the longer walks of the series and is mainly through the southern section of Gwydyr Forest, based on the small town of Penmachno. Because the route is over Forestry Commission roads and along some of the narrower lanes in the district, it is suitable for all weathers. This part of the forest is quite hilly but there are no really steep climbs involved, and the going for most of the way is fairly easy.

One part of the route passes through unfenced farmland where sheep are grazed. However, this is only a small proportion of the walk and providing dogs are kept under control on this stretch the remainder is suitable for dogs to be allowed to go loose.

Ty Mawr (Large House), a National Trust property lying in the little valley of the Wibernant, is a 16th century farmhouse where, in 1541, Bishop Morgan was born. He is famous in Wales for his translation of the Bible into Welsh. This had far reaching effects on the Welsh nation, in that it helped to weld together the different tribal groups of the country mainly by unification of the language, which, at that time, was split into several different dialects.

The start of the walk is in Penmachno. Parking is limited in the town. Cars can be parked on the outskirts, or the landlord's permission should be obtained to use the car park at the Machno Inn. The town of Penmachno and the village of Cwm Penmachno were both once thriving communities based on the slate industry. The huge quarries are now deserted (OS map ref. 751468) but are spectacular to see. The church at Penmachno contains some of the earliest inscribed Christian stones known in the country. These stones are thought to be sixth century in origin, and have on them the 'Chi-Rho' monogram used as a symbol by the early Christians.

Follow the road signposted to Ty Mawr for half a mile, then bear right at the fork and continue up the hill through stands of mature fir trees. This road runs up the hill for about 2 miles, and then comes out into more open country at about the 1000 ft level. Heather and bilberries are common up here, and so are lesser redpolls, and many other finches – chaffinch, goldfinch and linnet. A further stand of younger trees is reached; the trees here form a dark canopy which does not let much light through. The floor of the forest has, therefore, very little plant life growing in it. The road then runs downhill into the wooded valley of the Wibernant, past a café and a riding school and pony trekking centre. Ty Mawr is a few minutes' walk further on, on the left. It is open to the public.

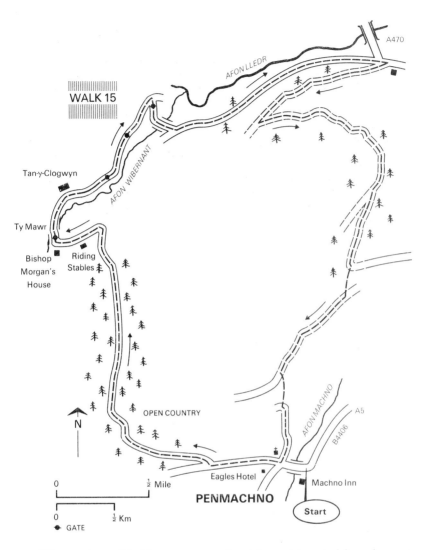

WALK 15

Tan-y-Clogwyn

Ty Mawr

Bishop
Morgan's
House

Riding
Stables

AFON WIBERNANT

AFON LLEDR

A470

OPEN COUNTRY

N

0   ½ Mile

0   ½ Km

GATE

Eagles Hotel

PENMACHNO

Machno Inn

AFON MACHNO

A5

B4406

Start

The road past Ty Mawr turns to the right and is gated from here on. This next stretch is grazing land and the road is unfenced. The Wibernant valley is a very pretty, unspoilt, little valley, with a small river running down it. The road runs alongside the stream, flanked by willows, sallow and alders. Reed buntings, grey wagtails and wood warblers can be seen here in the summer.

A second gate is reached and the road runs downhill on a long descent between dry stone walls. On the left are high crags. Foxgloves are very prolific. Tree pipits are very numerous on this stretch, the males continually flying into the air, then gliding down with out-stretched wings, singing. The road runs into the forest again. Turn

59

sharp right through a gateway. The Forestry road crosses the river and rises uphill. Keep on up the hill, alongside the river Lledr, and, after $1\frac{1}{4}$ miles, turn right at a road junction onto a Forestry Commission road which seems to double back up the thickly tree covered hillside. A mile further on, there is a Forestry Commission road to the left. This again seems to double back but winds up through the forest and over the hill, swinging round to the right. A fork is reached after a further $1\frac{1}{2}$ miles. Take the left hand road, which runs downhill slightly.

At the U bend $\frac{1}{2}$ mile further on, take the footpath on the right hand side through the forest. This leads straight on, and comes to another forest road. Bear to the right and follow the road and path down into Penmachno.

Walk 16
5½ miles (9 km)

Capel Garmon

Start: Capel Garmon, OS map ref. 815555

Capel Garmon is a village on the eastern side of the river Conwy and is in the small area of the Snowdonia National Park lying on that side of the river, between Llanrwst and Pentrefoelas on the A5. Archaeologically, it is famous for the well preserved chambered dolmen and this walk passes by the site of this Bronze Age tomb. Most of the walk is along the narrow lanes that characterize this side of the river valley and the uplands of Clwyd. It is easy going most of the way, and is suitable for any time of the year, especially winter.

There is only a short stretch of sheep grazing land and a farmyard to pass through – the rest of the walk being on narrow lanes which have very little traffic on them, even in the height of summer. However, dogs need to be kept well in hand.

Capel Garmon is reached by either turning off the A470 Llanrwst to Betws-y-Coed road or from the A5 road, the turn being about half way between Pentrefoelas and Betws-y-Coed. Both turns are signposted clearly. Park in the village, near to the White Horse Inn.

From the White Horse Inn walk through the village along the main street in a southerly direction. The burial chamber is signposted on the right hand side after about ½ mile. The way to it is well marked, along the entrance to Tyn-y-Coed farm and then across the fields. Guide pamphlets can be bought at the farm. This Bronze Age tomb was built between 2500–1900 BC and is unusual in that there are three chambers to it. It lies on an east–west axis. The original entrance is a narrow passage opening into the central chamber and runs from north to south. The roof of the three chambers was constructed of huge stone slabs, but only that over the Western chamber is now remaining. Eight upright stones support this roofing stone. The modern entrance to the tomb is now through the western chamber which has been used as a stable recently. The whole would have been covered by earth and stones. The area of the mound being indicated by a series of small stones. At the Eastern end a false entrance was built to confuse tomb robbers. It is possible that other mounds in this general area conceal as yet undiscovered and unexcavated chambers.

Having seen the burial chamber, continue past it across the field to a clearly visible kissing gate in the hedge. Through this gate keep slightly to the left and follow the edge of a wooded hillock. This swings around to the left after a couple of hundred yards. Cross the meadow to another wooded hillock, and bear right along the edge of this knoll. This will lead to a muddy stream and a cart track running off to the

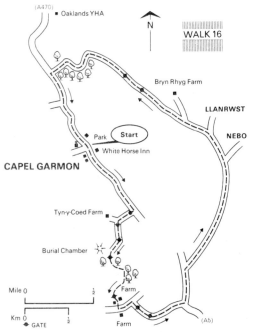

Bryn Rhyg Farm

LLANRWST

Park (Start

NEBO

White Horse Inn

CAPEL GARMON

Tyn-y-Coed Farm

Burial Chamber

Mile 0   ½

Farm

Km 0   ½
◆ GATE   Farm   (A5)

right. Follow this cart track down to a farm. The public path goes through the farmyard, past a green metal gate, and down to the road, which is not more than 100 yards from this gate.

Turn left along this road. After a short while it turns sharp right through a gate. There are fine views of the country southwards from here. The road is unfenced until it reaches a second gate. Carry on through, and at the next junction, turn left (OS map ref. 539826). A second road junction is reached after ¼ mile, and here turn right. This lane runs across the open fields for about 2 miles. The village of Nebo can be seen on the hill to the right, and at the next junction a signpost marks the road to Nebo, ½ mile away to the right. The left hand road leads towards Llanrwst; take it and within ¼ mile turn left up a smaller lane. Bryn Gwynog is on the left and, further up, the entrance to Bryn Rhyg farm. Carry on past this entrance, then past a gate across the lane, then through another. The surface of the lane becomes very broken after this as it starts to descend downhill through the woods. Eventually it comes out onto a narrow road. Turn left and after walking uphill for about ¾ mile Capel Garmon is reached.

For the botanist the lanes on this side of the river are full of interest, many unusual species being found. Bird life is much more of the agricultural type, many species of finches being quite common in this area – chaffinches, goldfinches, bullfinches, greenfinches, yellow-hammers, and linnets especially.

Walk 17   Capel Curig and the Ugly House

6½ miles (10 km)

Start: Tyn-y-Coed Hotel near Capel Curig, OS map ref. 733573
or Pont Cyfing, OS map ref. 735571

The river Llugwy flows down from the Carneddau to Betws-y-Coed,
joining up with the river Conwy there. Before it reaches Betws-y-
Coed, the river flows over the famous Swallow Falls. Telford's
London to Holyhead coach road, now the A5, follows the course of the
river up from Betws-y-Coed to Llyn Ogwen. This valley has some
beautiful scenery, and provides excellent walks. This walk takes in a
variety of country, the wooded valley of the Llugwy, the western
section of Gwydyr Forest and the open moorland behind Capel Curig.
It is a moderately strenuous walk, and certainly on the open stretches
of moorland and in parts of the forest good waterproof shoes or boots
are needed, as, even in summer, the going can be very soft and damp.
Providing good wet weather gear is available, it is suitable for all times
of the year.

Dogs are not recommended to be taken, as several parts of the route
have notices specifically saying dogs must be kept on the lead.

The start is at the Tyn-y-Coed hotel, on the A5 one mile outside
Capel Curig towards Betws-y-Coed. There is a very large car park
opposite the hotel which has an old stage coach parked in it. (This
coach was used in the making of the film *Jamaica Inn*.) This car park is
for hotel patrons only. Alternatively, the car can be parked at Pont
Cyfyng, ¼ mile down the A5 and on the small road to the right, when
driving towards Betws-y-Coed. Either parking place is satisfactory
from the point of view of this walk.

If a start is made at the Tyn-y-Coed hotel turn right on coming out
of the big car park and walk down the A5 for ¼ mile. On the right, just
opposite a grey-green painted telephone box, a road crosses a bridge –
Pont Cyfyng – and runs up past a small group of houses. This is where
the alternative car park is suggested. The Llugwy flows over some fine
falls and rapids just under the bridge.

Follow this narrow and quiet road for a couple of miles. Along this
stretch there are some beautiful woods – mountain ash, birch and oak
– which are at their best in the autumn. The Llugwy flows down
beside the road, curving away in places, and the A5 is on the far side of
this river. About 1 mile along, the Llugwy curves in to come close to
the road, then swings away again, and in the angle of this bend stands
the remains of the Roman fort – Caer Llugwy.

This small fort was not permanently occupied but is thought to
have guarded a crossing of the river, and also to have had some con-

63

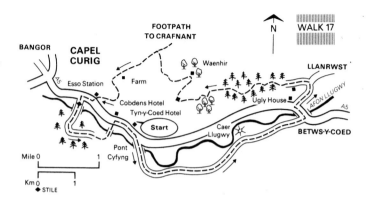

nection with the lead extraction from the area. Large quantities of lead ore have been found around the site: possibly the fort was a collecting point for the ore and stood guard over it, until shipment could be arranged.

The road meets the A5 again as the latter goes into a series of S bends. Turn left and cross the A5, taking care on the bends. Walk for 100 yards up the A5, then go up the small road to the right which goes past the Ugly House (Ty Hyll). This house, built in about 1475, is reputed to have been built in a night. In fact, there is an old custom that if between sunset and sunrise a person could build, without the landlord knowing, a chimney and fireplace, at least, and have a fire in the grate, the ground on which the house stood could be his, as well as that land which could be covered by a man standing at the front door and throwing an axe north, east, south and west. It is reputed that a band of brothers did this in one night and claimed the freehold, although, looking at the size of the stones used in building the chimney, it must have been a gruelling night's work.

Climb the very steep hill, past The Towers outdoor pursuits centre. After $\frac{1}{4}$ mile, a bridle track runs off to the left along the edge of the forest. There is a stand of firebeaters at the entrance to this bridle path. Follow it past a cottage, the track going uphill here. A wooden gate is reached, and on the other side a small stream. Cross this stream and bear left. Another cottage is passed and a stile leads into a fir wood. A second small stream flows across the path. The path then runs close to a wall with wire along the top and then comes out on a Forestry Commission road. Turn left and a short way further on at the junction of two Forestry roads, take the right hand branch. Not more than 50 yards beyond this T junction, a footpath runs down through the undergrowth to the left. Follow this down the valley.

This is a very marshy place, but the direction of the path is clear. A stream is reached with two wooden railway sleepers as a bridge, and the path bears round to the left slightly, rising up through the wood until it comes out onto an overgrown Forestry Commission road.

Keep to the left, uphill. This road, in turn, meets a well-kept Forestry Commission road after about $\frac{1}{4}$ mile. Keep to the left and follow this road for about $\frac{1}{2}$ mile until it comes to the edge of the forest. This stretch was devastated by a forest fire in the dry summer of 1976, and, as can be seen, is only slowly recovering.

At the end of the road (OS map ref. 738578) a footpath goes through the undergrowth. This, after a 100 yards, comes to a stile and out onto open moorland. At this point, the walker must pay close attention to the directions. The ground is very marshy and is relatively featureless. After crossing the stile follow the wall straight ahead until, after 100 yards, an open pasture is reached on the left. Cross into this pasture and, in the small valley below, a copse can be seen of willow and low oaks. Walk down the hill towards this copse and cross the marshy ground in the bottom of the valley. The path here is indistinct but sections of it are clear. Cross a stream, climb over a fence and climb up the small knoll. From the top of this knoll further open land can be seen ahead, with a fence running across it. About $\frac{1}{4}$ mile away there is a stile over the fence, and a clearly marked track running up towards Waenhir – a deserted and shuttered farmhouse, in a clump of trees – clearly visible to the right. Cross the stile and walk to Waenhir; the ground is very marshy even on parts of the track.

In front of the house there is a green; turn left here and walk up the cart track between two walls. This leads up over a hill, bearing slightly right. At the crest of the hill the path leads downhill again bearing slightly to the right. From this vantage point on the hill the Capel Curig to Crafnant path can be seen clearly in the small valley ahead, running off to the right. Walk down to this path and, when on it, turn left (southwards). Follow this track until it reaches some houses and keep on down the hill along the stony driveway, passing through a swing gate onto the A5 by a petrol station. Turn right along the A5 and then, almost opposite, go through a gate, onto a Forestry Commission road over a concrete slab bridge marked '10 ton weight limit'.

Walk into the forest and turn left at the T junction. This road runs alongside the Llugwy and at the point where it ends, a path continues by the river climbing over a rocky outcrop, and coming down to a footbridge. Cross this bridge, which comes out opposite Cobden's Hotel. The Tyn-y-Coed hotel is $\frac{1}{4}$ mile further on down the A5 to the right (or Pont Cyfyng, a further $\frac{1}{2}$ mile from Cobden's Hotel).

Walk 18   Capel Curig and Llyn Cowlyd

7½ miles (13 km)

Start: Capel Curig, OS map ref. 721581

The start of this walk is in Capel Curig itself. It is a fairly strenuous walk and like walk 17 goes over country that can be very soft and wet in places, even in the height of summer. Waterproof shoes or boots are certainly necessary. Waterproof gear should also be carried as parts of the walk are above 1000 ft and there is no shelter for long stretches across the open moorland.

The walker will find that the views from the route of this walk are some of the finest in Snowdonia, with the jagged peaks of Tryfan, Moel Siabod, and the Carneddau range all providing a feeling that this is the wildest of places. Llyn Cowlyd – a drinking water reservoir – is a large, 2 mile long lake set in the hills, surrounded by steep crags.

Dogs are not recommended as the walk goes across sheep country most of the way and the last stretch is along the busy A5 for a short distance.

The start is up the road leading past Joe Brown's Mountaineering shop, in the centre of Capel Curig, where the A5 and A4086 meet. Cars can be parked in the centre of Capel Curig, although space is limited.

Walk past the shop, through the gateway and along the road. This follows the course of the Llugwy, on the other side of the river from the A5. Across the valley behind the A5, the peaks of the Carneddau rise up: Carnedd Dafydd at 3423 ft (1044 m) and Carnedd Llewelyn at 3485 ft (1062 m) are not far below Snowdon's height of 3560 ft (1085 m). This old track continues for about 3 miles until it reaches a farmhouse and camp site.

Walk along the stony cart track in front of the farm and turn right down the driveway, across a cattle grid onto the A5. Turn right down the A5 and walk downhill for about ¼ mile. A Public Footpath sign-post points the way to the left up a cart track. A second signpost along the track points to a high wooden stile over a wall. Continue up the hill passing wooden posts acting as way markers. This part of the walk is extremely marshy, even on the path. The path climbs up behind a farmstead, Tal-y-Braich, and comes to a Water Authority leat, which is lined with rock and concrete. Follow the track to the right, climbing several concrete stiles towards a smooth-topped hill. The hill to the left is Pen Llithrig-y-Wrach 2623 ft (799 m).

A meeting of the waterways is reached and a wooden bridge is crossed leading off to the right (OS map ref. 705615). Follow the course of this waterway across the moor, in an easterly direction. The

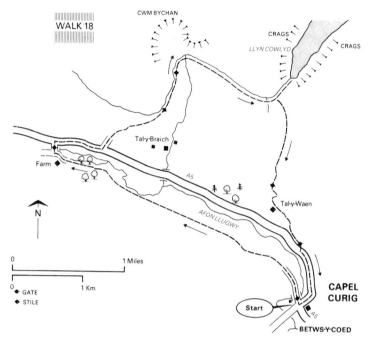

WALK 18

CWM BYCHAN

CRAGS

CRAGS

LLYN COWLYD

Tal-y-Braich

Farm

A5

AFON LLUGWY

Tal-y-Waen

N

0   1 Miles

0   1 Km
◆ GATE
◆ STILE

CAPEL
CURIG

Start

A5

BETWS-Y-COED

water is flowing eastwards, although the leat appears to run uphill. After a mile, a green shed is passed and another wooden footbridge is crossed. Llyn Cowlyd is about $\frac{1}{4}$ mile to the left. You may wish to walk down to the lake but, to return to Capel Curig, go right at the meeting of the tracks, close to the footbridge.

The path back to Capel Curig is marked by stakes set at long intervals, although the course of the path is fairly clearly defined. The going on this stretch of about a mile is very soft in places. A stile is reached and the route lies half right across a stream through a boggy patch, after which the course of the path becomes quite clear, running down just behind a small farmhouse – Tal-y-Waen. Fine views up the valley can be had, with Llyn Ogwen in the distance. Tryfan rises up to 3009 ft (917 m) in a jagged peak; just beyond it lies Y Gam at 3104 ft (946 m), whilst in a more southerly direction lie the Glyders at about 3280 ft (995 m). The whole view on a fine day is magnificent.

The path continues downhill and comes to Public Footpath gate onto the A5.

Left from here, it is $\frac{1}{2}$ mile downhill to Capel Curig. There is a narrow footpath beside the A5 which widens after a while, but walkers should keep well in, off the road.

Walk 19　　　　Cwm Idwal and the Devil's Kitchen

3¼ miles (5 km)

Start: Ogwen Cottage Youth Hostel, OS map ref. 648603

The other mountain walks described in this series provide the walker with wide views of open country and far distant ranges. This walk goes into the heart of the mountains, and the towering cliffs around the Devil's Kitchen seem to almost overpower and enclose the walker. Although relatively short, it is fairly energetic and needs good stout boots or shoes, warm clothing and waterproofs. It is not recommended, if icy or very wet conditions are prevalent, otherwise the walk can be undertaken at all times of the year.

Dogs are definitely not allowed within that part of the walk going through the National Nature Reserve and should be left behind.

Cwm Idwal lies at above 1200 ft but the Devil's Kitchen rises up to around the 2000 ft mark. Twll Du (the Black Hole) or the Devil's Kitchen is a deep vertical chasm in the rock face on the southern side of Cwm Idwal. Cwm Idwal is a valley that was formed during the ice age by the movement of glaciers.

Llyn Idwal is a shallow lake formed by the glaciers grinding a hollow in the rocks and leaving a dam of rock debris at the northern end of the cwm, so allowing water to collect. The area of the lake and cwm is a National Nature Reserve, as many rare mountain plants grow here, and the geology of the area is internationally famous. Idwal slabs are also a well known rock climbing face, as are all the crags in this area.

The start is from Ogwen Cottage Youth Hostel and Mountain Rescue Station on the A5 between Capel Curig and Bangor. There is a good sized car park here, and just down the main road there is a small tea kiosk, used by climbers and walkers.

From the car park climb the steps to the notice board. From here take the left hand path which leads over a stile and across a bridge. The roughly paved path to Llyn Idwal is clear to follow as it crosses the moorland towards the cliffs. This is National Trust land and the path has been paved to prevent erosion by walkers, for, the soft ground here is very liable to become worn away by continual usage. This path, after almost half a mile, reaches an iron gate leading into the Nature Reserve, controlled by the Nature Conservancy Council. The lake is directly ahead and the Devil's Kitchen and the Idwal slabs are at the far end of it.

Take the path to the left around the lakeside. This is well marked and relatively easy walking, but at the far end of the lake the path leaves the lakeside and starts to rise across the cliff face. It is still

68

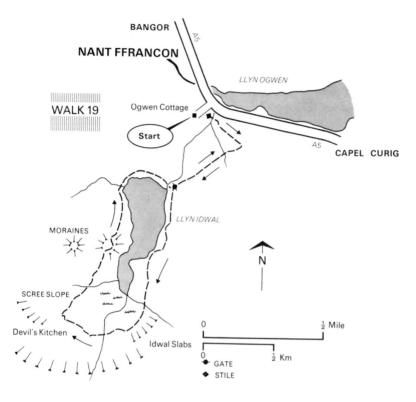

BANGOR

A5

NANT FFRANCON

LLYN OGWEN

|||||||||||||||||||||||||||||
WALK 19
|||||||||||||||||||||||||||||

Ogwen Cottage

Start

A5

CAPEL CURIG

LLYN IDWAL

MORAINES

N

SCREE SLOPE

Devil's Kitchen

Idwal Slabs

0   ½ Mile

0   ½ Km
● GATE
◆ STILE

---

clearly visible at this point, rising past the Idwal slabs, which usually have groups of climbers on them.

On reaching a point about level with the southernmost tip of the lake the path levels out. Go to the right and not upwards at this point. A small ravine is reached with a fast flowing river running down it. Scramble across this. After crossing this river the path continues to climb upwards towards the Devil's Kitchen, passing some fenced off trial compounds, which are used for testing the effects of sheep grazing on the mountain vegetation. The path runs round the lower corner of the compounds, then goes across to some very massive boulders. Scramble up through these, bearing right. Just here, the deep crack in the rocks known as the Devil's Kitchen is directly above the path. Proper climbing gear is needed to go higher into it.

At this point the path is not so clear. It starts to descend into a gulley. Although the way is quite safe, care should be taken here as it is on steep descents that the majority of mountain accidents happen. The lake and the path which runs alongside its western edge are clearly visible below.

Some scrambling is needed to get down the loose scree of small rocks and boulders, and also down some of the rockier parts of the descent. At the bottom, cross a river and rejoin the clearly marked track which runs alongside the lake. This is soft in places, and crosses a series of humpy little hills, which are glacial moraines – rock debris left by the glacier. At the north end of the lake, the route drops down to lake level before reaching the iron gate at the entrance to the Cwm Idwal Reserve. Follow the paved path back to Ogwen Cottage and the car park. On the way back there are good views of Llyn Ogwen, which lies across the A5 on the other side of the valley. A cup of tea can be had at the shelter a few yards down the A5.

Walk 20   Aber and the Menai Straits

8 miles (13 km)

Start: Aber Hotel, OS map ref. 651732

As a complete contrast to the other walks so far described, this one
follows the shore line of the north-eastern end of the Menai Straits
from Aber up to the entrance of the river Ogwen, and, after crossing
the A55, goes along narrow country lanes, which are in fact the old
route along the coast before the A55 was built. Bird watchers will find
this walk of great interest, the whole of the area known as Traeth
Lafan (Lafan Sands) and the entrance to the Ogwen being a notable
gathering place for many sea birds and waders.

The route is on the level for the whole of the shore line but after
crossing the A55 the road rises quite steeply, then runs along the hill
with very fine views of Anglesey and the Menai Straits. Walking along
the foreshore shingle can be quite hard going in places, so it is advisable to allow plenty of time to complete the round. It is a walk suitable
for all times of the year, but remember a cold wind comes off the sea in
the winter.

Dogs are free to roam, with the warning that the foreshore at low
tide is soft muddy sand and there is a short stretch along the very busy
A55. The lanes are all through sheep pastures but the walls and fences
are in good repair and there is very little traffic met with along them.

The start is at the Aber Hotel, this is reached by turning right off
the A55 at Aber when travelling from Conwy to Bangor – about 200
yards beyond the petrol station on the left, or, if coming from Bangor,
then turning left at the bottom of the short hill past Bangor
University's College Farm. This road, which is a continuation of the
Roman road across from Bwlch-y-Ddeufaen and Roewen, runs down
towards the shore and after about $\frac{1}{4}$ mile forks, take the right fork and
park beside the road, near the Aber Hotel. Go back to the fork. Turn
right down the other road and pass under the railway. This lane leads
down to the flat shore of Traeth Lafan. A footpath signpost points to
the left and right. Take the left hand route. Follow the cart track and
where this leads up to a farm bear right and walk along the foreshore.
This is loose shingle with rocks in places and, although flat, can be
quite hard going. The salt marsh plants are very interesting, sea asters
and sea rocket, in particular being plentiful. At high tide, or near to it,
there are hundreds and sometimes thousands of waders to be seen,
oyster-catchers, curlews, redshank, dunlin, knot and plovers. Rarer
waders such as godwits, spotted redshank and greenshank are also
regularly seen at the spring and autumn migration times. In summer
sandwich terns are common. Traeth Lafan at low tide is an area of

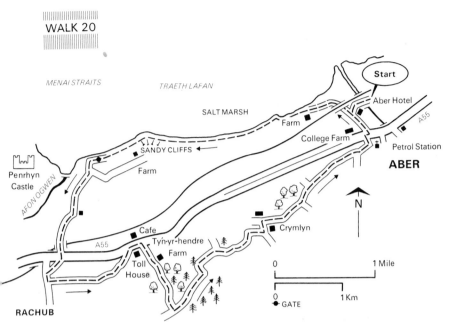

MENAI STRAITS · TRAETH LAFAN · SALT MARSH · Farm · College Farm · Start · Aber Hotel · A55 · Petrol Station · ABER · SANDY CLIFFS · Farm · Penrhyn Castle · AFON OGWEN · Cafe · Tŷn-yr-hendre Farm · Toll House · Crymlyn · N · 0 · 1 Mile · 0 · 1 Km · GATE · RACHUB · A55

about 7 square miles, and in early times was the route taken at low tide to get to Anglesey, a short sea crossing being made across the Straits at Beaumaris. It is a well known area for cockles and clams, and, in places, large patches of bleached white clam shells, can be seen. The live clams and cockles live just buried in the sandy mud of the sands. The shore line does not have many other sea shells apart from mussels.

After about 1½ miles muddy cliffs rise up, which are obviously being rapidly eroded away, judging from the newly fallen trees at the bottom of them. It is unusual, also, to see elm trees growing virtually on the shore. Penrhyn Castle comes into full view on rounding a small promontory. This is a late Georgian castle built in the Norman style around 1830. Although still lived in, it is now under the care of the National Trust and is a spectacular place to visit to see the furniture, carpets and carvings, as well as the railway exhibition.

Before the castle, the Ogwen river runs into the Straits, and before this leave the foreshore, walking onto a rough patch of ground which leads into a lane running away from the shore. This lane runs down beside a perimeter wall and wood on the right, passing a couple of farms on the left. After a mile, the A55 is reached. Bearing right across the road go up the lane, almost opposite, signposted to Rachub. 100 yards up this lane turn left and walk down a lane that runs parallel with the A55. This, in fact, was the old route to Bangor before the A55 was built. The houses fronting the road indicate this.

The lane rejoins the A55 on a bend at a Toll House. Across the road there is an old cottage now used as a café, and about 200 yards on another lane leads off to the right. Take this lane and walk up past Ty'n-yr-hendre farm. The narrow lane comes into a patch of woodland and goes up a very steep hill. At the top a T junction is reached. Turn left and walk along the lane running across the side of the hill. There are some spectacular views here of the coastal plain, the Straits and Traeth Lafan, as well as Anglesey and Puffin Island. The lane eventually descends to the little hamlet of Crymlyn. Turn right at the T junction and walk for a further mile until the A55 is reached at Aber, just opposite College Farm.

Cross the A55, bearing right and go down the road on the left which, after about $\frac{1}{2}$ mile, comes to the fork near the Aber Hotel where the walk started.

Walk 21   Aber Falls

3 miles (5 km)

Start: car park at Bont Newydd, south of Aber village, OS map ref.
663720

This is one of the shortest walks included in this book. It is easy going,
on well marked paths, but being almost entirely through sheep
grazing country is not really suitable for dogs. Although short, the
walk is very scenic and there is a fine view of the Aber Falls at the
furthest point. The path runs up the valley of the Afon Rhaedr, which
is rich in oakwoods on either side, as well as passing several bogs, with
associated insects and plants. The bird life is also very typical of an
oakwood valley and species are seen frequently here that are not so
abundant elsewhere in the area. It is a pleasant walk at all times of the
year, especially after heavy rain when the falls are at their most
spectacular.

The start is reached by travelling along the A55 from Conwy to
Bangor, and at Aber turning left into the small village, immediately
beyond the Aber Falls Hotel and petrol station. The road then bears
right and heads up the valley until a car park is reached, close to the
river at a place called Bont Newydd. On the other side of the river
there is a wooden Nature Conservancy building and exhibition. A
nature trail (Coed Aber) is also laid out by the Nature Conservancy
Council, leaflets about this trail being available from the exhibition.

After leaving the car park pass through the gate and walk alongside
the river for several hundred yards. This brings one to a footbridge;
cross this and pass through the gate on the far side. A cart track leads
up to the right, along the line of the valley. Eventually a small cottage
is reached, and, from here, the track becomes a footpath. This part of
the walk is interesting because of the marsh plants that can be found
in the boggy patches of willow scrub close to the track. Marsh
marigolds, or kingcups, are common and provide a welcome touch of
colour in the spring. Frog spawn can often be found in the marsh in
the early spring and, overhead, ravens, buzzards and curlews are frequently to be seen. By the river, grey wagtails, dippers, and parties of
warblers, tits and goldcrests are common. Further up the valley as the
path goes through patches of oaks, pied flycatchers, redstarts,
nuthatches, tree creepers and wood warblers are often present in the
summer, providing a selection of oakwood species not often seen by
people from outside the area.

On reaching the falls, there are fine views of the distant hills, as well
as of the falls themselves.

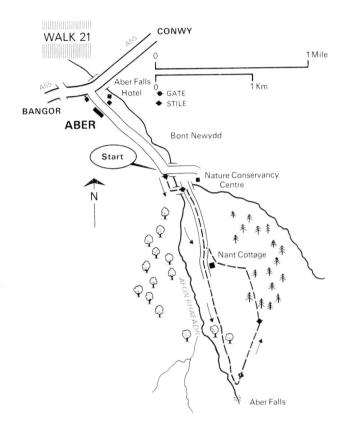

WALK 21

CONWY

A55

Aber Falls
Hotel

● GATE
◆ STILE

0 _____ 1 Mile
0 _____ 1 Km

BANGOR

A55

ABER

Bont Newydd

Start

N

Nature Conservancy
Centre

AFON RHAEADR

Nant Cottage

Aber Falls

On the return, keep to the right diagonally up the hillside, to a stile over a wire fence. Keep going diagonally across the hillside towards the edge of a Forestry Commission wood. Enter the wood and follow the path through it, which keeps close to the edge of the trees. This path is not used a great deal and there is a good chance of seeing not only jays and sparrow hawks, but also some animals, such as foxes, stoats, squirrels and even polecats. A gate is eventually reached which opens out onto the hillside, and the path then goes down to the track originally taken on the way up, and so back to the car park.

Walk 22 Dolwyddelan and Carreg Alltrem

4 miles (7 km)

Start: Dolwyddelan station, OS map ref. 738522

The Lledr valley runs from Betws-y-Coed up towards Blaenau Ffestiniog. The Afon Lledr, together with the Llugwy and the Conwy join near Betws-y-Coed all flowing northwards to Conwy and forming the Conwy river. Nowadays the A470 road and a single track railway run down the valley to Blaenau Ffestiniog, but in the old days this was an important pack horse route, and it is thought that Dolwyddelan Castle was built in the twelfth century not only to prevent marauders passing up the Lledr valley but also to guard this important trading route. The valley itself has a different character from the Llugwy or Conwy valleys, being more wooded and 'softer'.

This walk runs southward from Dolwyddelan through the big Forestry Commission plantation beneath the crags of Carreg Alltrem and Foel Fras. It is a very pleasant easy going walk which could be known as the Water Walk as the route never seems to be far from the sound of running water. There are no problems at any time of the year.

Dogs can be taken, as the whole length of the route is on Forestry Commission or public roads.

To reach the start drive to Dolwyddelan and, if coming from Betws-y-Coed, after passing Elen's Castle Hotel on the right, turn left down the road to the Station. This is a wide street and the car can be parked here or in the old station yard by the school. The station is now only a single platform and shelter, trains only stopping on request.

From the station walk over the bridge to the left and keep left. 100 yards further on, a Forestry Commission gated road runs off to the right. Follow this road along the side of the hill into the plantation. The trees here have been thinned once, so are not too thick, and there is enough light between them to provide a certain amount of undergrowth. Coal tits, jays, and sparrow hawks may be seen. Further on the road forks, take the right hand road. This crosses a series of small streams and goes past an open, marshy area on the right. This has a small river flowing down it and an old slate slab bridge crossing it. The sallows and willows here are excellent cover for many birds. Herons, in particular, find the area a good hunting ground. Very large dragonflies are common.

Carrying on through the pine forest, a much larger open space is reached. The whole view from here is reminiscent of the Tyrol or Switzerland, with a fertile open valley having a couple of farms in it, surrounded by steep-sided mountains covered in dark green forest,

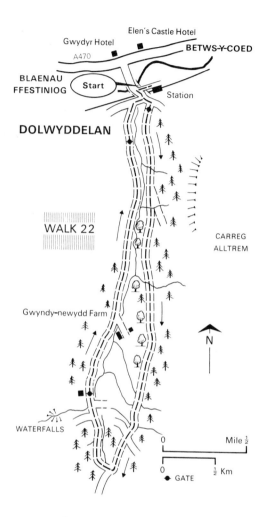

WALK 22

with a river running down the centre of the valley. It is a very peaceful scene: the crags of Carreg Alltrem on the left, with Foel Fras ahead and a fine waterfall coming down the hill. On the far side of the narrow valley are the cliffs of Craig Tan-y-Bwlch.

Walk along the road which runs the whole length of the 3 mile long cwm or mountain valley. Several small streams cross the road, running off Carreg Alltrem. At the next crossroads keep straight on, the road then circling around to the right. It is noticeable that the rocks at this end of the valley are much more 'slatey' in type and, in fact, Blaenau Ffestiniog with its huge slate quarries lies only 3 miles away on the far side of Foel Fras.

77

A ruined cottage is passed on the left. At the next fork, keep right, the road coming into the open. Soon there is a gate across the road, and after this a large house appears on the left. This has been a farm but is now used as a week-end or summer holiday home. The road changes from being stone surfaced to tarmac, passing down the western side of the valley.

A ruined farm is passed, then a row of ruined cottages where miners once lived. The walls here are all built of flat slatey pieces of rock, as are the cottages, which are mostly of dry stone construction, with a minimum of mortar. The road runs beside a fast flowing, clear river.

After passing through a further patch of forest, the road comes into open country. Dolwyddelan can be seen below, and behind Dolwyddelan the huge mass of Moel Siabod.

Downhill, a gate is passed, and then the outskirts of the village are reached. Bear right along the road, which leads to the station after a quarter of a mile.

Walk 23

6¼ miles (10 km)

Roman Bridge and
Llynau Diwaunedd

Start: car park at Hafod Gwenllian, OS map ref. 717512

Walk 22 commenced in Dolwyddelan and ran southwards from there. This one covers another part of the Lledr Valley. It is moderately easy going but crosses some very wet patches of country and good waterproof shoes or boots are recommended, especially in the winter.

Llynau Diwaunedd are twin mountain lakes set in the heart of the hills, surrounded by steep-sided mountains, the far end being in the shadow of Y Cribau (1940 ft, 591 m). The walk provides interesting contrasts, with the river valley and woods and pastures being compared with the starker country of the higher hills.

Dogs are not recommended to be brought on this walk as, although about half is through forest plantations, on the other sections there are notices specifically forbidding dogs.

The start is reached by driving down the A470 from Betws-y-Coed to Blaenau Ffestiniog. Driving westwards through Dolwyddelan, about 2 miles beyond Elen's Castle Hotel, a Forestry Commission car park at a place called Hafod Gwenllian is reached on the left. This takes about six or seven cars. There is also a picnic site laid out here, close to a small river flowing down to the Lledr.

From this car park cross the A470 and walk down the lane opposite, marked with a cul-de-sac sign. This road winds down the valley close to the single track railway line. Roman Bridge Station is passed. It is unmanned now, the trains only stopping if waved down. The road runs up over a hill, which provides a viewpoint of the Lledr valley beyond, backed by the heights of Yr Arddu (1966 ft, 589 m) and Moel Meirch (1998 ft, 609 m).

From here it curves round to cross the Lledr at Pont-y-Coblyn (Bridge of the Goblin). The river is very shallow here, but grey wagtails, sandpipers and herons can often be seen. At the far side of the bridge, a public footpath sign shows the way across a meadow. This path is paved with stones, which are very useful in the wet weather. It swings left and runs up the hillside to meet the road, opposite a white painted farmhouse.

A public footpath sign at the other side of the road shows the way through the farmyard. The track has been well paved all the way up the hill here and was clearly of some importance at one time. Further on it passes across a meadow and the paving is lost, but 100 yards or less ahead on the other side it is possible to pick it up again. The ground here is very damp and even by making use of the paved track it is difficult to avoid the marshy patches.

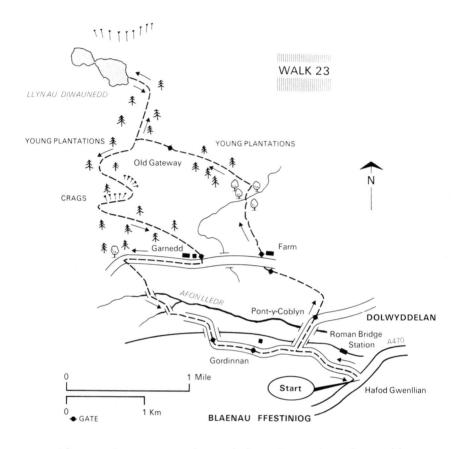

LLYNAU DIWAUNEDD

YOUNG PLANTATIONS

Old Gateway

YOUNG PLANTATIONS

N

CRAGS

Garnedd

Farm

AFON LLEDR

Pont-y-Coblyn

DOLWYDDELAN

Roman Bridge
Station   A470

Gordinnan

0   1 Mile

0   1 Km
◆ GATE

Start

Hafod Gwenllian

BLAENAU FFESTINIOG

After crossing a very marshy patch the path runs through a scrubby wood of birch, sallow and low oaks. Cross a small river on the stepping stones. From here the path rises out of the wood and comes into a newly planted area of conifers. Through this plantation the path tends to bear left and becomes indistinct in places. It rises fairly soon above the 1000 ft mark and the country becomes progressively wilder and bleaker compared with the Lledr valley. The path then reaches a plateau, and the remains of a gateway with wooden posts. A forest track through the plantation goes left and, after $\frac{1}{4}$ mile, reaches a newly made forest road.

Turn right here. Llynau Diwaunedd can be seen ahead, partly hidden by a small hill. Y Cribau and Clogwyn Bwlch-y-Maen lie straight ahead. The road leads down to the lakes, which can be bleak in bad weather but pleasant in summer.

On the return, retrace the route up the forest road and instead of turning off at the point where it was joined on the way out, keep on along it. This road winds in a series of long loops downhill towards the Lledr valley.

After about $1\frac{1}{2}$ miles from the point where the outward track joined the new road, the small hamlet of Garnedd is reached. Climb the gate and join the lane. Several of the houses are now deserted and clearly the whole area was far more populated fifty to a hundred years ago. Various ruined houses can be found all along this road. Most of the former inhabitants worked in the slate industry.

From here, two routes can be taken to return to the Hafod Gwenllian car park. The shorter one is to turn left, and walk along the lane for about $\frac{1}{4}$ mile to the point where the public footpath originally crossed it going down to Pont-y-Coblyn on the way out. The slightly longer route is to turn right, walking past the chapel down to the point where a wood is reached on the right, with a derelict house in it. Opposite, a grass track runs across the field. This leads past a small slate spoil heap to a footbridge over the river. After crossing the river, climb the fence, and walk across to another footbridge over the Afon Gordinnan, clearly visible in the middle of the next pasture. After crossing the second footbridge follow the track up to the railway bridge. This is dated 1894, indicating how relatively recent this section of the railway line is. Turn left over the bridge and follow the cart track past Gordinnan farm onto the public road which leads to Roman Bridge station and the Hafod Gwenllian car park.

Walk 24

4½ miles (7 km)

The Pass of Aberglaslyn
and Cwm Bychan

Start: car park near the Royal Goat Hotel, Beddgelert, OS map ref. 589481

Walks 24 to 28 are all in the region of Beddgelert. This village lies to the south-west of Snowdon and is in the shadow of Moel Hebog (2566 ft, 782 m). Being on the southern side of the great mountain mass around Snowdon, the Glyders and the Carneddau, the country is very different in character from the northern part of Snowdonia and the Conwy valley. The lower hills are 'softer' in character and they are more broken up into small valleys often filled with rhododendron thickets and bushes.

There are some fine walks to be had in this area. This one takes in Aberglaslyn Pass, a noted beauty spot, where the river Glaslyn has cut a gorge through the hills. It is moderately easy going at first, but later the route climbs fairly gently up Cwm Bychan and then across the top of the hills, and there is then a steep descent on the other side, back to Beddgelert. Although the first half is along well made paths and tracks, the last half is over rougher hill country which can be very damp in places. Good boots or waterproof shoes are recommended, as well as waterproofs. A compass is also useful. With this equipment the walk is suitable for all times of the year, but should not be attempted in its entirety if visibility is very bad.

All the walk is through sheep grazing country and dogs need to be kept under control the whole way. For this reason, it is not really recommended that dogs be taken.

The start in Beddgelert village is from the public car park near to the Royal Goat Hotel. Beddgelert is reached by turning off the A5 at Capel Curig and driving down the A4086 and A498. This is an extremely spectacular 12 mile drive in itself. Alternatively the A4085 can be taken from Caernarvon, or, if coming from the south, take the A498 road from Porthmadog.

From the car park turn left and walk back through part of the village. Before reaching the road bridge over the river, turn right along the path marked to Gelert's grave. Gelert was the faithful hound of Prince Llewellyn killed by his master by mistake after defending the prince's baby against an attack by a wolf. This small road runs beside the river up to a footbridge. A short diversion can be made to walk to Gelert's grave – a stone cairn, about ¼ mile away – this path going to the right just before the footbridge. The route for the walk, however, is over the bridge and then turning right to follow the course of the river Glaslyn. This is a well marked path, over paving stones and a stile. It

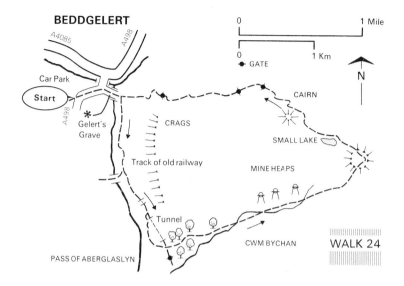

BEDDGELERT

A4085   A498

Car Park

Start

A498

* Gelert's Grave

0   1 Mile

0   1 Km
◆ GATE

N

CAIRN

CRAGS

SMALL LAKE

MINE HEAPS

Track of old railway

Tunnel

CWM BYCHAN

WALK 24

PASS OF ABERGLASLYN

reaches the course of the old Welsh Highland Railway, now completely dismantled. The track bed running through the Pass of Aberglaslyn makes a good route for walking.

Walking along the track beside the river southwards, as the Pass is approached, so the wooded cliffs close in and the river becomes more wild and spectacular. The old track passes through several cuttings in the rock and a short tunnel, then comes to a larger tunnel. This tunnel can be walked through quite safely, but as it takes a right hand bend in the middle and is about ¼ mile long the centre part is quite dark. The surface is reasonably smooth and providing one goes slowly and carefully this stretch is quite safe. For those who don't like dark places, it is possible to go down to the river side and scramble along the rocks at the edge of the river, a narrow little path being found there. This route involves crossing a small log bridge, made of old telegraph poles. Dippers are common on this stretch of the river – unmistakable black and white thrush-sized birds bobbing up and down on the rocks in the river.

At the far end of the tunnel, there is a path running left up the hill, the track of the old railway keeping straight on.

For a shorter walk, by keeping on the railway track, a return to Beddgelert can be found which leads back down the far side of the river.

The route for the main walk runs up left from a few yards beyond the exit to the tunnel. This path rises gently up Cwm Bychan. This small valley seems always to be warm, filled with oak, birch, mountain ash and sweet chestnut trees, and with a river running down it with crystal clear water. This cwm typifies the country south-west from Snowdon. On the right the pyramidal shape of Cnicht rises up.

The path continues to rise up the cwm. It is well marked and becomes grassy. The remains of old mine workings are found soon. At the head of the valley, copper was mined and there are trial workings all the way up – rusty brown spoil heaps and trial working entrances to be seen running into the hillside. Do not go into these.

The small gantries for carrying the iron buckets are still in place up here, mementoes of earlier times, and a different way of life for the local men. Most of the derelict equipment is now hidden in the bracken and gorse. The path criss-crosses the river several times and then continues up past the final turntable for the mining gantries.

Beyond this point, the path comes to a grassy, flat, bowl-shaped area surrounded by low rocky hills. Behind, there is a fine view of the cwm with Tremadoc Bay beyond.

At this point, the way becomes difficult to find and it is important to follow the route instructions carefully. Go up the left side of the grassy bowl, onto the lip. At the ridge on top, a small lake is seen below. Take a route which runs down past the lake and across to the far side of it. Do not take the path which runs along the hillside to the right.

Cross the grassy area on the other side of the lake, entering a small shallow valley which runs in a westward direction. At the head of this shallow, grassy valley, keep straight on, and within a couple of hundred yards a small cairn will be seen on top of a rock. Walk up to this cairn, and from here head northwards downhill. Beddgelert village will be visible in the valley below, also Beddgelert Forest and, on a clear day, in the far distance the Snowdon Horseshoe. It is suggested that if the visibility is poor, a compass should be used. On no account wander too far to the left (or south-westwards) from this cairn over the top of the hill.

A clearly marked track running downhill to the left will be met with, about 200–300 yards from this cairn. This runs fairly steeply down the hill, curving round to a gate in a stone wall, and then continues on down. Some scrambling is needed in places but the path is quite clear. A white farmhouse in the valley below is a good guide to aim for.

The path comes to a grassy saddle with another path clearly visible running along it. Walk down to this path and go down the hillside to the outskirts of the village. The path goes through a gate onto a service road and past a public footpath notice. Turn left here and then cross the little green to the footbridge over the river and so through the village to the car park.

Walk 25

Nantmor

4½ miles (7 km)

Start: Nantmor, OS map ref. 601460

___

Nantmor is a small village to the south of Beddgelert. Nantmor means sea valley and is a reminder of the time when the sea came up the flat valley to the south. Two hundred years ago an embankment was built at Porthmadog and so this area was claimed from the sea.

The walk is an easy one along pleasant narrow lanes and through oakwoods. The going is good all the way and the walk is suitable for all times of the year.

Long stretches are along little used lanes but parts are through open sheep country and a small farmyard is crossed. Dogs should be kept well under control, if taken.

Nantmor is reached by driving out of Beddgelert on the A498 to Aberglaslyn Pass. At the river bridge turn left down the A4085, and about ¼ to ½ mile further on Nantmor is signposted to the left. Park in the village of Nantmor.

Walk out from the village keeping along the same road that was used to come in by. This lane winds up and down hill, through woods and past a Forestry Commission plantation.

After a mile, a road junction is reached. Turn left by an old slate roofed cottage and walk up through the woods of Coed Caeddafydd. Go past Cae Ddafydd pottery and after a further mile, a picnic site beside the river is reached. This is a pleasant, sunny spot, and makes an enjoyable stopping place.

Just past the picnic site, there is a gate across the lane. A hundred yards past this gate, a break in the stone wall on the left shows the way down across a field to a wooden footbridge across the river (OS map ref. 621468). From here, the path runs across the field to an old stone barn near a wood. Head for the opening at the left hand end of the barn.

From here, the stony path climbs through the oakwood, joining another track coming from the right. Bear left. A meadow is reached. Keep on the wood side of the stone wall; the path then crosses this wall into the meadow. Pass through the wooden gate that can be seen directly ahead. Bear slightly left up a hillock, joining a cart track coming from the left, after about 200 yards. Follow this track along the shallow deserted valley, through the meadows and birch trees. This is the haunt of buzzards, redstarts and many small woodland birds.

A group of ruined cottages is reached. The cart track swings away to the right across the little valley before reaching the cottages, and

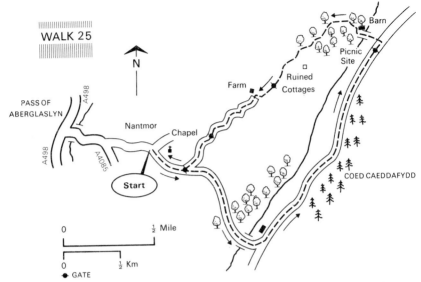

PASS OF
ABERGLASLYN

Nantmor

Chapel

Farm

Ruined
Cottages

Barn

Picnic
Site

COED CAEDDAFYDD

Start

N

0   ½ Mile

0   ½ Km

◆ GATE

goes uphill. Following this, the stony track comes out into a meadow
at the top. From here, turn left and walk across the meadow to a white
painted metal gate. Through this gate the path rises up the hill to the
entrance to a small farmyard, passing in front of the farmhouse. A
notice here says 'Mowing grass, keep to footpath'. Go through the
yard and down the access road (OS map ref. 612464).

This metalled lane runs downhill for a mile, passing a small group
of cottages and then coming out on the Nantmor Road. There is a
white gate across the access road here.

Turn right and walk the mile back to Nantmor.

Walk 26   Croesor and Sarn Helen

5 miles (8 km)

Start: Garreg, OS map ref. 612418

It is possible on this walk to enjoy a pleasant afternoon along some
very beautiful lanes up to Sarn Helen, the old Roman trackway from
Caernarvon to Caerleon in South Wales, returning through the forest.
Alternatively the trip can be extended for a $8\frac{1}{2}$ mile walk which follows
the lanes covering a triangular piece of the country based on Croesor,
Garreg and Tan-y-Bwlch. Both routes are easy going over undulating
country, with only short stretches of steep hill. The longer route is best
undertaken outside the high season of June to August to avoid road
traffic.

The shorter walk is suitable for all times of the year, especially for
the spring and autumn. Dogs are also able to run loose. On the longer
route, however, the third side of the triangle is along the B4410, which
can have a lot of tourist traffic on it in the summer.

The start of the walk is at Garreg. This is on the A4085 road from
Penrhyndeudraeth to Caernarvon. Garreg is a small village about 3
miles north of Penrhyndeudraeth. Cars can be parked in the village,
off the main road.

From the Brondanw Arms at Garreg walk up the A4085 for $\frac{1}{4}$ mile.
An arched gateway with a lodge over it is reached, together with a
signpost pointing to Croesor. Turn right up this narrow road past the
lodge. There are thick woods here, and the lane goes uphill past
Plasbrondarnw and various other buildings of the estate, which are of
a different style from those usually found in this part of the country.
Ffynon Gwyfil (the spring of Gwyfil) is passed on the right hand side.

This road through pleasant wooded hill country runs for $2\frac{1}{2}$ miles
up to Croesor. It is fairly straight, although undulating, for the whole
way except for the last $\frac{1}{2}$ mile when it bends sharply and rises steeply.
At the crossroads, turn left and walk up to the small village of Croesor.
Sarn Helen runs through here on its way southwards from
Caernarvon. Passing a car park and a bridge over a river the lane
climbs up a steep hill, then down again to a metal gate and wooden
stile. Over the stile a rough paved road (Sarn Helen) leads up through
the woods. This surface must have been much the same when it was
used in Roman times. On the left, 30–40 yards up the hill from the
gate, there is a small mossy opening at the base of the wall. This is the
original Ffynon Helen, or Spring of Helen. The legend attached to
this place is that one hot day Empress Helen, the Welsh born wife of
the self-proclaimed Emperor Magnus Maximus, was travelling

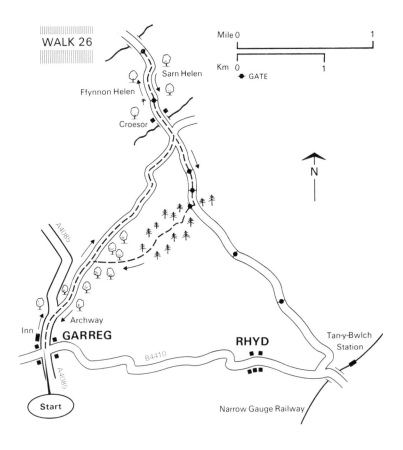

WALK 26

Mile 0   1

Km 0   1
                    ● GATE

N

Sarn Helen

Ffynnon Helen

Croesor

Inn
Archway
GARREG

RHYD

Tan-y-Bwlch
Station

B4410

A4085

A4085

Start

Narrow Gauge Railway

southward from Caernarvon with a party of Roman soldiers. The rear guard was commanded by her favourite younger son. The Empress rested to drink from this spring after the hot climb over the hill behind, but shortly afterwards a runner came up to tell her that the rear guard had been ambushed and that her son had been killed by an arrow, possibly shot by his jealous elder brother. She cried out in Welsh 'Croes awr' (sometimes translated as 'O cursed hour'). From this cry of anguish, many years later the village of Croesor, took its name and the spring became known as Ffynon Helen. Nowadays very little water flows from it, as the main flow of water has been diverted by the Water Authority to an underground storage reservoir for supplying drinking water to the village.

Continue up the paved track, passing a footpath going off to the right, until the top of the hill is reached. Sarn Helen then drops downhill through a gate to a bridge built of huge slabs of rock across a small rushing river. This is a good spot for a rest or a picnic.

Return to Croesor, and to the crossroads – about 15 minutes' walk from the stone bridge – and continue straight over. This way is marked to Tan-y-Bwlch. The lane is through open country and has several gates across it. At the point, where a Forestry Commission plantation starts on the *right* hand side, there is a gate. Go through this if you are taking the shorter route. On the other side the Forestry Commission road runs through the wood, bearing to the left. This comes out into open country and runs steeply downhill to another small wood. A short distance through this wood, the lane above Plas Brondarnw is reached. Turn left and walk back to Garreg along the same route.

For the alternative, longer route, do not enter the Forestry Commission plantation but keep walking along the lane. This comes finally to a point very close to Tan-y-Bwlch station on the narrow gauge railway from Ffestiniog to Porthmadog. A hundred yards further down, the lane reaches the B4410. Turn right and walk for $2\frac{1}{2}$ miles along this road to Garreg, going through the village of Rhyd on the way.

Walk 27

Beddgelert and Moel Hebog

5½ miles (9 km)

Start: car park near the Royal Goat Hotel, Beddgelert, OS map ref. 589481

The mountain of Moel Hebog lies to the west of Beddgelert and dominates the village. At 2568 ft it is not one of the highest peaks in the area, Snowdon being almost 1000 ft higher, but its ascent is rewarding and this is one of the most energetic walks of the series. The path is clearly marked all the way to the summit and providing the route instructions are followed the way is quite safe. At the top, on a clear day, there are views for miles across the mountains and the southerly and western coast line of Snowdonia. Because of the height climbed, plenty of time should be allowed for this walk, certainly four hours, and most probably longer if full enjoyment of it is to be had. Some scrambling is needed on the last section, but this is quite easy and certainly no rock climbing is involved. Providing good waterproof boots or shoes are worn and adequate protective clothing is taken the walk should be suitable for all times of the year, except when there is snow or ice on the peak, or in very misty conditions. A compass is very useful as it will help to identify from the map many of the different peaks and places that can be seen from the summit

Dogs are not recommended to be taken, as most of the way is through open sheep country, and the last part of the ascent of Moel Hebog is very rough walking for dogs

The start, which is the same as for Walk 24, p. 82, is from the main car park in Beddgelert. This is off the A498, close to the Royal Goat Hotel.

Coming out of the car park, turn right towards the Royal Goat Hotel and walk through a group of modern houses. A public footpath signpost shows the way to a path leading up between some of the houses. This comes to a stile and a meadow. The path crosses the meadow to a wall, and further on a steel gate on the right leads through into a wooded pasture. There is a signpost here 'To Cwm Cloch'. Walk across this meadow, bearing slightly left, and go through a stone flanked gateway. The track here can be seen quite clearly crossing the meadow. Pass the edge of a small copse on the left. The copse has had a barn built in it at one time, but this is now ruined. Keeping on this way a gate in a dry stone wall is reached, which has beside it a notice pointing back the other way marked 'Beddgelert'. Through the gate, a road is reached. Turn right, and continue along this grassy road, past some old farm buildings to Cwm Cloch farm.

At the farm, a stile will be seen on the left. Over the stile, the

WALK 27

BEDDGELERT FOREST

STONE WALL

Old railway track

School

GRASS SLOPE

Cwm Cloch Farm

Car Park

Royal Goat Hotel

BEDDGELERT

SHEER CRAGS

SCREE

MOEL HEBOG (782m)

N

A4085

A498

A498

Start

GATE
STILE

0   ½ Mile

0   2 Km

pathway leads across some damp pastures to another stile. From this point up to the summit of Moel Hebog the route is marked all the way by cairns. The ascent is basically in three sections, the earlier one being to Cwm Cloch farm, the middle one being up to the point where a scree slope starts before the summit, and the final section being up the scree slope to the summit. The centre section of the ascent, whilst being steep, is over grassy country and, in places, soft ground. By taking the ascent in easy stages it is not too arduous, but it is best not done against the clock. It is also advisable to pick out the next cairn route marker before leaving the previous one, especially on the last section, where some easy scrambling is required. Some of the cairns nearer the top are quite small but if the next is located each time there is no chance of losing the way up. From the top, where there is a large cairn, there are some fine views, not only across the mountains eastwards, but southwards to Porthmadog and the Glaslyn estuary, and westwards to the Lleyn peninsula and Anglesey.

The first part of the return is down the same route. It is important to descend by this route until the base of the high precipitous crags on the left is reached. From here, strike out across the grassy slopes towards Beddgelert Forest. These slopes, although steep in places, have no unexpected crags or falls in them. Moving down them half right, head for a dry stone wall. This wall has a river running down beside it. At about $\frac{1}{4}$ mile from the forest edge, there is a low point in the wall. Cross the river and the wall and carry on down on the other side. A corner of the forest boundary is reached, where there is a stile over the wall. On the other side, the path leads down the hill, until, just after a blocked up opening in the wall, the path swings away left into the forest. Continue to follow the path downwards. It reaches the end of a Forestry Commission road, but go down past this road.

91

Further on, the path comes out at the meeting of two more Forestry Commission roads. Go straight across both these and keep on downwards. Here the path runs beside some meadows on the left, then swings around to the right, shortly afterwards meeting another Forestry Commission road. Turn left down this road, until a T junction is reached, then turn right here. This is the track bed of the old Welsh Highland Railway and runs into Beddgelert, passing through clumps of rhododendron bushes, birch, and mountain ash. It provides a good even walking surface. A diversion has to be made to the left at one point, however, and use made of the lane leading onto the main A4085 Beddgelert to Caernarvon road. Turn right along the footpath and walk down to the school. Cross the footbridge and turn left. The car park is only a couple of hundred yards from here through the housing estate.

Beddgelert has plenty of cafés, inns and hotels in which to recover, if needed.

Walk 28   Beddgelert Forest

8 miles (13 km)

Start: Rhyd-Ddu, OS map ref. 572525

The country north of Beddgelert provides excellent walking routes. This walk covers a good variety of terrain, from marshy pasture land to forest roads and footpaths. The southern flank of Snowdon is less spectacular than the northern and eastern sides but the long grassy slopes provide wide views of the country and give a sense of space.

The walk is long but easy going and can be attempted at all times of the year. Parts of the walk are very wet and certainly good waterproof boots or shoes are necessary, as well as adequate wet weather clothing. The central section is through Beddgelert Forest where dogs can roam freely but otherwise the route is across sheep country and in the first half dogs are specifically asked to be leashed.

The start is from the small village of Rhyd-Ddu on the A4085 Caernarvon to Beddgelert road. There is a large car park with toilets here, and it is in fact the starting point for one of the ascents up Snowdon.

From the car park cross the A4085 and take the path marked by a public footpath notice. This leads across a marshy meadow, but the way is made drier by the provision of paving stones. The path leads behind a white cottage, over a footbridge and stile and then rises up the hill towards the B4418 road.

At this road, on the left, another path is marked crossing the low-lying country around Llyn-y-Gadair. This route is marked 'To Pennant'. The muddy track runs along beside the wall, over a stile, then bears left. The route is marked with white arrows and is quite clear. From here it crosses some very wet and marshy ground towards Beddgelert Forest. At one point, a small river is crossed and after this a wide bog. By keeping uphill at this point the way through the bog is slightly drier. Continuing along this path a gate into the forest is reached.

In the forest, the path shortly leads down to a Forestry Commission road. Carry straight on, past a notice saying 'To Dolbenmaen'. A road to the right is passed, then the road swings round to the left, meeting up with another road. Turn right and take a path on the left signposted 'To Dolbenmaen'. This path winds uphill through the forest, passing patches of open ground, then going back into the forest. Finally after a good climb on a paved trackway the path comes into the open with a view of Moel Hebog and Moel Lefn, then, on coming around the shoulder of the hill, Tremadoc Bay and the Lleyn Peninsula come into view.

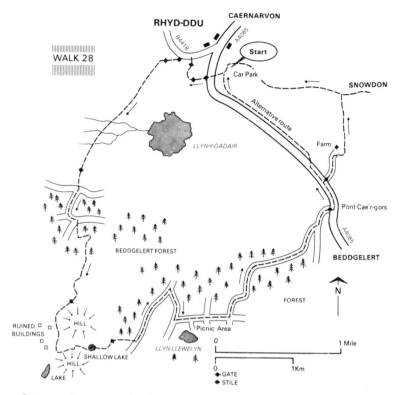

It is very important for the next section to take particular note of the route directions.

Pass through a wooden gate out of the forest area into sheep pasture. At the other side of this gate bear left downhill towards a couple of ruined quarry houses. Go past these, taking the track downhill to the left past a long row of ruined quarrymen's barracks. After about 100 yards a path branches off to the left down the steep little slope, heading towards the shoulder of the high hill on the left.

Follow the path over the shoulder and between two hills (OS map ref. 551498). There is a small lake in the valley below on the right. This is rocky ground but easy going. On the other side of the shoulder lies a small shallow marshy lake. In dry conditions, rather sporadically placed stepping stones allow the walker to cross without getting too wet, but, in wetter times, it is better to work round the lake on the higher ground and alongside the wall. The path then leads up between stone walls, coming to a slate slab stile. This leads back into the forest. Follow the rather marshy path through the trees downhill until a Forestry Commission road is reached. Turn left.

After about $\frac{1}{4}$ mile, a small lake can be seen through the trees on the right. Just after this a plot of trees will be passed on the left, commemorating the discovery in Wales of the hybrid *Cupressocyparis leylandii* (Leyland cypress). This fast growing hybrid is now a popular

94

hedging tree in gardens. $\frac{1}{2}$ mile further on, turn right down another Forestry Commission road, then at the bottom of the hill turn left to pass the small lake, Llyn Llewelyn. There is a pleasant picnic area here.

Keep straight on past a red and blue marker post. At the next crossroads, go straight across, then at another crossroads, turn left. This road bends to the right, then left downhill. Ahead the smooth slopes running up to Snowdon can be seen (OS map ref. 566508). After crossing a couple of streams the road bears to the right and then goes through the forest along a straight stretch; it then bears to the left to the Pont Cae'r-gors forest exit.

Coming out onto the main A4085 road turn left and walk along it for about $\frac{1}{4}$ mile. From here there are two alternative routes. The longer, but more interesting one, is to turn right into the entrance to a farm, where there is a notice clearly marked 'Public Footpath to Snowdon'. Follow this driveway up to the farm, bearing right past the farm itself and walk up the hill for about $\frac{1}{4}$ mile. The track from Rhyd-Ddu is reached. Turn left down this path back to the car park. The shorter, though possibly less pleasant, route is to walk the whole way back to the car park along the A4085, using the trackway of the old railway for the last $\frac{1}{2}$ mile.

Walk 29   Llanberis

5 miles (8 km)

Start: Llanberis, OS map ref. 578599

Llanberis, like Blaenau Ffestiniog, is a town which grew up with the boom in the slate industry in Victorian times, and in the country park area on the eastern side of Llyn Padarn relics of this industry can be seen in the museum. The walk gives a good view of the huge operation involved in this slate quarrying, as well as fine views of Llyn Padarn and the mountains beyond. Llanberis, nowadays, is the lower terminus for the Snowdon Mountain Railway, and, on fine days, Snowdon can be seen towering up to the south.

The route is mostly over well surfaced tracks and lanes, but there are stretches across very boggy country and good waterproof boots or shoes are essential. There is a short stretch where some easy scrambling is required over the old slate quarry debris, otherwise the going is reasonably smooth, the last section being entirely downhill.

Dogs are not recommended on this walk because of the sheep and because the way passes across very soft ground and rough edged slate spoil.

The start is in Llanberis itself, which lies off the main A4086 Caernarvon to Capel Curig road. Park in the town close to the large church with a square tower.

A side road runs southwards in front of the church, and between it and the lake. Walk up this small road which winds uphill. A public footpath notice on the right shows the way through an iron swing gate, up some steps. This path bears left, past a stone barn and through the woods, coming out onto a track. Turn left, then after a few yards only bear right. From here, on the far side of the lake, the slate works can be seen. Llanberis slate is a beautiful purple colour, and different from the greyer Blaenau Ffestiniog slate.

The path comes out after a short way onto the road running up by the Snowdon Mountain Railway. Just across the trackway of the railway there is a view point of some fine waterfalls. But returning to this side of the railway turn right, uphill, coming to a notice saying 'Heol Breifat, Llwydyr Cyhoeddus, Public Footpath Only'. Walk up here and bear left past the entrance to a pottery. From here a track running to the left between two low stone walls will be seen (OS map ref. 577592). Follow this uphill. The land here is very marshy. At the end of the walls the course of the track can be seen running across the mountain pasture, bearing slightly right. After about $\frac{1}{4}$ mile this comes to an iron gate onto a stony road opposite a small electricity sub-station building. Snowdon can be seen clearly from here slightly

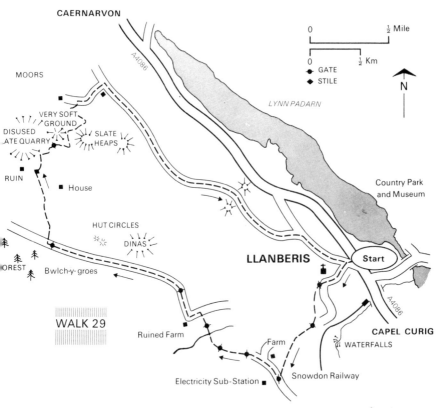

MOORS

VERY SOFT
GROUND
DISUSED
SLATE QUARRY
SLATE
HEAPS

RUIN

House

HUT CIRCLES

DINAS

FOREST

Bwlch-y-groes

WALK 29

Ruined Farm

Farm

Electricity Sub-Station

LLANBERIS

Start

LYNN PADARN

Country Park
and Museum

CAPEL CURIG

WATERFALLS

Snowdon Railway

0   ½ Mile

0   ½ Km

● GATE
◆ STILE

N

to the left, and the route of the railway can be followed by the smoke
from the steam engine as it puffs up the side of the mountain.

Turn right along the stony road, passing a small farm. At this point,
continue straight on, going through a gateway with an iron gate
across it. Follow this track across the hills passing through several
gates. Just after the last gate, the track meets a metalled lane. Turn
left uphill and go past a derelict farmhouse. At the top of the rise, the
hill fort of Dinas comes into view on the right together with some
abandoned slate workings. In the pasture at the base of Dinas are
several hut circles, but they are not easily seen unless searched for.

Along this track about ½ mile after the derelict farm, a newly
planted forest comes into view ahead. Before this forest is reached,
there is a gate. Go through this gate and turn sharp right along the
wall, and across the hill pasture. It is most important that the directions for the walk should be carefully followed for the next section,
both for keeping to the public right of way and for safety.

Keeping along the wall, follow it to the far end, where, close to a
derelict house, an iron stile bars the way. Go over the stile (OS map

97

ref. 556604) then cross the pasture half left to the base of some slate spoil heaps. Follow the wall seen ahead down the low slate spoil heaps, to an iron gate in the wall. (Ignore the roughly blocked up way through the wall, a few yards uphill from this gate.) Climb the gate and continue to follow the wall downhill. At the point where the wall turns to the right strike out across the heather half right down the slope. After a hundred yards more slate quarry debris is reached, and at this point a cart track through the debris can be seen going downhill to the left. Follow this track down around the base of the larger spoil heaps, and after a couple of hundred yards down the track, the route goes out directly across the moor past some thorn bushes. This is a very damp area. From here cross to the base of another spoil heap and keeping to the base of this heap go downhill until a slate wall is reached. At this wall go left, keeping close to it for $\frac{1}{4}$ mile across some very boggy country.

After passing a further slate heap open country is reached. Ahead lies a small farm. Keep beside the wall until it turns to the left. Climb it at this low point, passing through a gap in the wall on the other side and follow this other wall down hill until reaching the track running up to the farm. From here, turn right and follow the track downhill to where it meets a metalled lane, with grass down the middle.

Turn right and walk for about $1\frac{1}{2}$ miles downhill to Llanberis, passing some very deep parts of the quarry, now disused. Entering Llanberis, walk down Rhos Olg, Yankee Street, Rock Terrace, Bryn Teg and so to the High Street, which then comes to the church.

Walk 30   Snowdon

8½ miles (13 km)

Start: Pen-y-Pass Youth Hostel, OS map ref. 646556

This walk is one of the most energetic of all in the series, Snowdon at
3560 ft being the highest mountain in England and Wales. From
Llanberis there is a steam driven train which goes to the Summit, but
it is far more satisfying to walk up by one route and down by another.
There are, in fact, several routes up to the top starting at widely
different places. This walk, however, follows the route up the Miners'
Track from Pen-y-Pass car park, and then returns down the Pyg track
to the car park, at Pen-y-Pass.
   In both directions, the going is fairly steep, and the average time
that should be allowed is 2½–3 hours up and 2–2½ hours down.
Certainly good walking shoes or boots need to be worn, as well as
warm and weatherproof clothing, even on the warmest days. Both
routes are quite safe providing the path is kept to and the ascent is not
attempted in icy or very thick misty conditions. The views on the way
up and down are magnificent and from the summit, on a clear day,
places as far away as Ireland, the Isle of Man and Cumbria are visible.
Unfortunately the summit is fairly often obscured in cloud, but this
cloud generally, in good weather, is only for the last few hundred feet,
so it is possible to obtain views across most of Snowdonia all the way
up to the cloud line.
   The walk should not be attempted in very low cloud or icy conditions. Dogs can be taken if kept under control but the ground is very
rough and rock strewn with steep falls quite close to the path, and is
not really suitable for dogs running loose.
   The start is at the Pen-y-Pass Youth Hostel which is on the A4086
Caernarvon to Capel Curig road. It is close to where the A498 road
from Beddgelert joins the A4086. At this point, the height above sea
level is 1160 ft (356 m). A fee is payable for use of the car park.
   The Miners' Track leaves the car park at the far end. It is a broad
path, well paved with stones, and in earlier times was used by the
miners and the mine company to get to the Britannia copper mine
which is about half way up Snowdon near Llyn Llydaw. Initially this
track provides good walking and only a gentle climb. Moel Siabod is
clearly seen on the left and so is the wooded Gwynant valley running
down towards Bedgellert. As it swings round the shoulder of the hill,
Y Lliwedd, Crib-goch, Snowdon and Crib-y-ddysgl all come into
view. These famous peaks go to form the Snowdon Horseshoe a forbidding semicircle of sheer cliffs.
   Llyn Teyrn lies on the left, with the ruins of some of the miners'

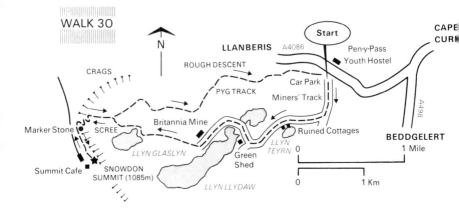

N

LLANBERIS A4086

Start

Pen-y-Pass
Youth Hostel

CAPE
CURF

ROUGH DESCENT

CRAGS

PYG TRACK

Car Park

Miners' Track

Britannia Mine

Marker Stone   SCREE

Ruined Cottages

BEDDGELERT

LLYN
TEYRN 0

1 Mile

LLYN GLASLYN

Green
Shed

A498

Summit Cafe   SNOWDON
SUMMIT (1085m)

LLYN LLYDAW

0   1 Km

barracks by its shore. Shortly afterwards Llyn Llydaw comes into view. Keep right at the green valve-house and cross the causeway between the two lakes. This causeway was built by the miners in 1853. The lake is 190 ft deep and on a sunny day has quite a blue tint, indicating the presence of copper in the water.

Across the causeway the track follows the far side of the lake to the left. This is still easy going and pleasant walking. The old mine buildings of the Britannia mine are reached, and from here the path starts to ascend more steeply.

At the top of this stretch, Llyn Glaslyn is reached. This lake is 126 ft deep and lies at the base of the Snowdon Horseshoe. The water in this lake is a strong blue colour, and this is a very wild and remote place, surrounded by the crags of Snowdon. The croaking of ravens only adds to the air of remoteness. There are more ruined miners' barracks here. The miners lived here during the week, and returned home by the various paths at the weekends.

The path follows the shore line of Llyn Glaslyn, then branches off right up the steep scree slope. This is one of the steepest parts of the climb, and from here, on a clear day, the tiny figures of other walkers slowly moving up the mountain ahead look quite unreal.

At the top of this slope the Pyg track is joined coming from the right. Both tracks continue up to the left, climbing steeply and winding up the crags. The track goes into a zig-zag, some scrambling is needed here. Eventually a large marker stone is reached at Bwlch Glas, close to where the track meets the Snowdon Mountain railway up from Llanberis. The summit station is about a further 15 minutes' walk up from here, and the actual summit marker is a very short distance further up to the left.

The café at the top has a refreshment room, toilets, and a gift shop.

To return, follow the course of the railway down to the Bwlch Glas marker stone. From here descend the zig-zag to that point where the Pyg track leads away to the left along the base of Crib-y-ddysgl and Crib-goch. This is quite an easy junction to miss when on the way down. The Pyg track can be seen running along the hillside and appears quite level, but in fact it is fairly rough going. This track keeps up high for some way then swings behind some high ground and falls away quite steeply down towards Llanberis Pass. Looking back the lakes at Llanberis can be seen, and, after a while, the Pen-y-Pass Youth Hostel comes into view some way ahead. The going here is quite hard, some scrambling being needed down the rocky steps and boulders, but it becomes easier for the last $\frac{1}{2}$ mile, before reaching the car park.

Glossary

This list of Welsh words is intended to help the walker understand the place names which are mentioned in this book and others which may be encountered while on the walks.

Aber	Mouth
Afon	River
Allt	Hillside
Bach	Small
Betws	Small church, oratory
Bod	House
Bont	Bridge
Bryn	Hill
Bwlch	Pass
Bychan	Small
Cader	Seat
Cae	Field
Caer	Fort
Capel	Chapel
Castell	Castle
Cefn	Ridge
Cerrig	Rocks
Coch	Red
Craig	Rock
Croes	Cross
Derwen	Oak
Dinas	Fort
Dulas	Dark stream
Dwr	Water
Eglwys	Church
Fach	Small
Fawr	Large
Ffordd	Road
Ffridd	Mountain pasture
Ffynon	Spring, well
Foel	Bare hill
Fras	Prominent
Garth	Hillside
Gelli	Copse
Glas	Green, blue
Glyder	Heap
Gors	Bog
Groes	Cross

Gwern	Marsh
Gwyn	White
Hafod/Haffoty	Summer dwelling
Hen	Old
Hendre	Winter dwelling
Hyll	Ugly
Isaf	Lowest
Las	Green, blue
Llan	Church, village
Llech	Slate
Llechwedd	Hillside
Lletty	Shelter
Llwyd	Grey
Llyn	Lake
Maen	Stone
Maes	Field
Mawr	Large, great
Melin	Mill
Melyn	Yellow
Morfa	Soft marsh
Nant	Stream or valley
Penmaen	Rocky headland
Pennant	Head of a valley
Pistyll	Waterfall
Plas	Large house
Rhaeadr	Waterfall
Rhiw	Hillside
Rhos	Marsh, moor or heath
Rhudd	Red
Sarn	Paved road
Tan	Under
Traeth	Shore
Ty	House
Tyddyn	Smallholding
Uchaf	Highest
y	the, of the
yn	in
Ynys	Island
Ysbyty	Hospice
Ysgol	School

Place names can be translated thus:

Betws-y-Coed	Small church in the wood
Penmaenmawr	Great headland of stone
Cae Coch	Red field
Hendre Isaf	Lowest winter dwelling
Sarn Helen	Helen's road